America's Living History

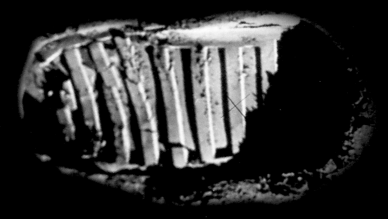

Space Race

The Mission, the Men, the Moon

Tom McGowen

Enslow Publishers, Inc.
40 Industrial Road
Box 398
Berkeley Heights, NJ 07922
USA

http://www.enslow.com

Copyright © 2009 by Tom McGowen

Library of Congress Cataloging-in-Publication Data:

McGowen, Tom.

Space race: the mission, the men, the Moon / Tom McGowen.

p. cm.—(America's living history)

Includes bibliographical references and index.

Summary: "Discusses the United States' role in the space race in the 1960s, including the beginning of NASA, early space exploration, and the first Moon landing by American astronauts"—Provided by publisher.

ISBN-13: 978-0-7660-2910-1

ISBN-10: 0-7660-2910-7

1. Space race—Juvenile literature. 2. Astronautics—United States—Juvenile literature. 3. Astronautics—Soviet Union--Juvenile literature. I. Title.

TL793.M395 2009

629.45'40973—dc22

2007051615

Printed in the United States of America

10 9 8 7 6 5 4 3 2 1

Illustration Credits: Associated Press, pp. 17, 19, 26, 52, 59; Getty Images, p. 95; The Granger Collection, New York, p. 10; NASA, pp. 1, 29, 38, 62, 78, 84, 94, 110; NASA, Apollo, p. 67; NASA, David Scott, p. 73; NASA, Edwin E. Buzz Aldrin, p. 100; NASA Headquarters-Greatest Images of NASA (NASA-HQ-GRIN), pp. 48, 86, 96, 101, 106; NASA, Kennedy Space Center (NASA-KSC), pp. 4 (top), 80, 98; NASA, Marshall Space Flight Center (NASA-MSFC), pp. 4 (bottom), 8, 21, 33, 56, 112; NASA, Russell L. Schweickart, p. 74; © POPPERFOTO/Alamy, p. 105.

Cover Illustration: NASA (footprint); NASA Headquarters-Greatest Images of NASA (Buzz Aldrin with flag).

Contents

view of the Earth appears over the lunar horizon (top) as the Apollo 11 Command Module comes into view of the Moon. The image at the bottom was transmitted to the world on July 20 1969, as Neil Armstrong climbed down to the lunar surface to become the first man on the Moon.

Chapter 1

The sky was total blackness—a night that never ends. Yet, the ground glowed in bright sunlight. It was a brownish-gray landscape of rocks and craters of all sizes extending as far as the eye could see. The gray ground and the black sky came together sharply in the distance in a long curving horizon.

Squatting on the rocky ground was a large machinelike object that looked like it was made of metal boxes and rods stuck together. From the bottom of the object stretched four long, slender, metal tubes, the ends of which rested on the ground. From an opening on the upper part of the object, extended a metal ladder, its bottom hanging about three feet above the ground. On the bottom rung of the ladder stood a man, his body entirely enclosed in a bulky white space suit, his head in a large round helmet, the front of which gleamed like gold. After a moment, he stepped from the ladder to the landing pad and then to the ground.

A man was standing on the Moon!

The Moon: A Source of Wonder for Thousands of Years

For thousands of years many people dreamed of a human going to the Moon. At the beginning of history, many

What Is the Moon?

The Moon is actually nearly a quarter of a million miles beyond Earth's atmosphere, in the vast black, airless region we call space. The Moon is a ball of rock, without air or water. It is the kind of object known to astronomers as a satellite, a small body that circles around a larger body, in what is called an orbit. Man-made objects in orbit are called artificial satellites. The Moon is kept in orbit by its own gravity and the Earth's gravity. Gravity is the force that pulls objects together and holds them in place. It is because of gravity that getting from Earth to the Moon is so difficult. To get to the Moon, a vehicle must travel fast enough and with enough power to overcome the force of gravity and get into space.

ancient people believed that the glowing silvery disk in the sky was a god or goddess. This belief later faded out, and people began to think of the Moon as a *place*, a strange and wonderful place that might somehow be visited.

Of course, there was no way for people to get up into the sky, where they thought the Moon was. Writers and dreamers began to think about ways humans might get to the Moon. About fourteen hundred years ago, the Greek writer known as Lucian wrote a tale of a sailing ship that was carried to the Moon by a whirlwind. This could not happen, of course, but in the story it gave Lucian a way of getting people to the Moon.

Finding a Way to Get to the Moon

Throughout the centuries, dreamers continued to imagine voyages to the Moon. The great German astronomer Joannes Kepler wrote a book published in 1634 about a trip to the Moon made by means of magic. In 1865, the French science-fiction writer Jules Verne wrote a book titled *From the Earth to the Moon*. The story tells how a group of explorers are sent to the Moon inside a projectile moving at tremendous speed, fired from a gigantic nine-hundred-foot-long cannon. This is not practical, but it shows how well Verne understood that tremendous speed and power would be necessary.

In 1883, a Russian schoolteacher named Konstantin Tsiolkovsky figured out how humans actually would get to the Moon. Tsiolkovsky was the person behind the theory of the rocket engine, the kind of engine that now powers all spacecraft.

The Rocket Engine

Rockets were invented in China, some time in the 1200s. They were powered by solid fuel, a flammable powder. They were used both as fireworks and as weapons, shot into enemy cities to start fires.

A liquid-fuel rocket engine is based on the same idea as a solid-fuel rocket. A solid-fuel fireworks rocket contains a charge of a highly flammable powder in its tail. When the powder is lit, it burns rapidly and emits gases in a burst of energy that pushes down toward the ground. A push in one direction causes a reaction in the other direction. If a person wearing rollerblades faces a wall and pushes forward on the wall he or she will roll backward.

The Chinese use rockets against the Mongols in 1232 in one of the earliest recorded instances of a rocket attack. The Mongol attackers fled in terror, even though the rockets were relatively harmless.

The push of energy from the back of a solid-fuel rocket makes the rocket go up into the sky. Konstantin Tsiolkovsky worked out the mathematics that showed how large and long a burst of energy would have to be to push a vehicle free of Earth's gravity and into space. Fireworks rockets use a substance similar to gunpowder for their energy burst, but Tsiolkovsky knew that was not powerful enough. He believed the best kind of fuel for a space-rocket engine would be a high-energy liquid, such as gasoline, that can produce an intense burst of power.

Robert Goddard, America's Rocket Engine Builder

Tsiolkovsky never actually tried to build a liquid-fuel rocket engine, but an American named Robert Goddard did. In about 1909, Goddard, a college student, became interested in trying to use a rocket to lift a vehicle into space. Like Tsiolkovsky, he believed that only a high-energy liquid fuel would work. He began testing different mixtures of liquid fuels. By testing fuels in airtight chambers with all the air pumped out of them, he proved that liquid fuels would burn perfectly well in the airlessness of space.

In 1926, Goddard, then a professor of physics, built and launched the world's first rocket powered by liquid fuel, a mixture of gasoline and liquid oxygen. The rocket moved at a speed of sixty miles an hour and reached a height of 41 feet.[1] He continued similar experiments through the 1920s and 1930s, always trying to send rockets higher and higher. By 1935, he had sent a rocket a mile and a half into the sky at a speed of seven hundred miles per hour.[2]

In 1919, Goddard's experiments drew the attention of newspapers. They wrote that he seriously hoped to send a rocket to the Moon. "Rocket ships" became

Robert Hutchings Goddard, fourth from left, and assistants L. Mansur, A. Kisk, C. Mansur, and N. L. Jungquist hold the rocket used in a flight on April 19, 1932.

important elements in comic strips and movie serials of the 1920s and 1930s. Science-fiction magazines such as *Amazing Stories* contained tales of men in "rocket ships," making visits to the Moon and planets. However, most people in America simply laughed at the idea of a "rocket ship" that could take a person to the Moon. Many people with little knowledge of science regarded Goddard's experiments as a waste of time, but many scientists and industrialists thought they were very important.

Chapter 2

In Europe in the 1920s and 1930s, people regarded the idea of rocket ships very seriously. One German college student named Hermann Oberth produced designs for workable rocket ships very much like those that later went into space. Another young student, Wernher von Braun, worked with a group known as the Spaceflight Society. These people were interested in building and testing rockets powered by liquid-fuel engines. They hoped to produce a rocket that could achieve spaceflight.

Von Braun's Rockets Become a Secret Weapon

The tests made by the Spaceflight Society started to interest the German army, which began to supply money and material to continue the tests. The army was looking for a way of making long-distance bombing raids. Some high-ranking officers hoped that von Braun's group could create a rocket engine capable of carrying a bomb through the sky for hundreds of miles to an enemy target. The work of von Braun and his group became a secret German military project in 1934, and continued in secret when World War II began in Europe, in 1939. By September 1944, Germany was facing defeat by the

The Weapon That Went to Space

Hoping to turn defeat into victory, Germany began using the super-secret weapon that von Braun had produced. Known as the V-2 rocket, this forty-six-foot-long cylinder with a tapering nose contained one ton of high-explosive material.[1] It was powered by a rocket engine fueled by kerosene and liquid oxygen that enabled it to travel about two hundred miles at a speed of about four thousand miles per hour.[2] The rocket was launched in a roaring explosion of flame that sent it arching up into the sky on a curving path that reached a height of sixty miles—the beginning of space. Then it hurtled down to explode in a shattering blast.

allied armies of the United States, Britain, and the Soviet Union, which consisted of several Eastern European countries led by Russia.

During the last months of World War II, more than twenty-five hundred of these rockets rained down on London and the Belgian city of Antwerp. They killed thousands of people and turned whole city blocks into piles of rubble. However, the rockets could not prevent Germany's defeat. On May 7, 1945, Germany's armed forces surrendered and World War II was over in Europe.

Von Braun Comes to America

When World War II ended, the two most powerful nations in the world were the United States and the Soviet Union. They both tried to get as much information about the German V-2 bombs as they could, so they could produce such weapons for themselves. They wanted to get their hands on the man who had been the brains behind the V-2 rocket, Wernher von Braun.

However, von Braun was not in the least interested in building better rocket bombs. He knew that the rocket he had created could be turned into a *spaceship*. He and his assistants wanted to keep on working to build a vessel that could actually go into space. They knew that both the Americans and the Soviets would be delighted to have their help and knowledge. Because the United States was regarded as the world's leader in technology, von Braun and his team believed their best chance of getting to do what they wanted lay with America. On May 2, 1945, five days before Germany surrendered, von Braun and his followers turned themselves in to the American forces in Germany.

But von Braun was to be disappointed. When he was taken to the United States, he quickly discovered that most American government and military leaders, as well as most ordinary Americans thought spaceships were silly fantasies out of comic strips. Instead of building a spaceship, von Braun and his team were employed by the U.S. Army to build engines to make faster rocket weapons with longer ranges.

Seeking Super-Weapons for the "Cold War"

Von Braun and his team were not the only scientists who had been working on rocket bombs for Germany during the war. There were others, and they had all been rounded up by Soviet forces and taken to the Soviet Union. Now, they were working to build improved rockets for the Soviet army.

The United States and the Soviet Union had been allies against Germany during World War II, but in only a few years they had become enemies. As the 1940s ended, the two nations were pitted against each other in what was called the "Cold War." Both sides knew open warfare could break out at any moment. The United States and Soviet Union were building liquid-fuel rockets as weapons to use against each other if war should happen. Both nations were trying to produce rockets that could travel thousands of miles, carrying atomic bombs—weapons that could cause incredibly powerful explosions by splitting the center of certain kinds of atoms. Such rockets were known as intercontinental ballistic missiles (ICBMs), explosive missiles that could travel from one continent to another. The United States and Soviet Union were in a "race" to be first to produce an ICBM. The one that got an ICBM first would have a big advantage, with the ability to make a bomb attack that the other could not prevent or strike back against.

The Soviets Put an Artificial Moon Into Space

In 1955, the chief Soviet rocket designer told the Soviet leaders that he would have an ICBM ready for launch in 1957. An ICBM would not only be powerful enough to carry a bomb thousands of miles, it would also be powerful enough to escape Earth's gravity and fly into space. The Soviet leaders decided that instead of just showing off that they had an ICBM, they would use it to do something that would show the world the scientific and technological power of the Soviet Union. They would use it to put something into space.

Meanwhile, in the United States, Wernher von Braun was working on a V-2-type ICBM that he called the Jupiter-C. It was tested on September 20, 1956. The nose cone went three thousand miles, coming down into the Atlantic Ocean at a speed of sixteen thousand miles per hour.[3] That was almost fast enough to get it into space. However, the U.S. government was not interested in spaceflight. It just wanted ICBMs.

On the night of October 4, 1957, a rocket was launched from the Soviet republic of Kazakhstan. With flame spurting from its rear, the rocket moved upward, eventually reaching a speed of nearly five miles per second near the edge of space. At a height of 142 miles, the rocket's cone-shaped nose was automatically separated from the body. An object inside the rocket was set free to continue rushing into space. This object was a 23-inch-wide, 183-pound metal ball containing a transmitter to send radio signals back to Earth.[4] Although it was in space, there was still enough of Earth's gravity pulling at it to keep it from traveling in a straight line. It went into orbit, beginning to circle Earth.

The Soviets had created the world's first artificial satellite, which the Soviets had named *Sputnik*, the Russian word for "co-traveler." It would now circle Earth every ninety-six minutes at a speed of eighteen thousand miles per hour.[5]

When news of *Sputnik* was released, the world went wild with admiration. Many Americans were stunned. They had believed that no other nation could match their science and technology. But now they had been "shown up" by the Soviets, who had dramatically demonstrated that their technology was ahead of America's. The Soviets had also shown that they had an ICBM that could probably send an atomic bomb to the United States. In a newspaper interview, a prominent scientist at the University of Chicago commented, "it cannot be denied that the United States has suffered a defeat. It was probably the defeat of the decade."[6]

Wernher von Braun had been working for the U.S. Army. Now, he believed his chance to launch a spacecraft had come. To keep pace with the Soviet Union, the United States would need a rocket that could put a satellite into orbit. Von Braun knew that he and his team had produced one—the Jupiter-C. He told a high government official that he and his team could put a satellite in orbit in sixty days, and begged to be "turned loose."

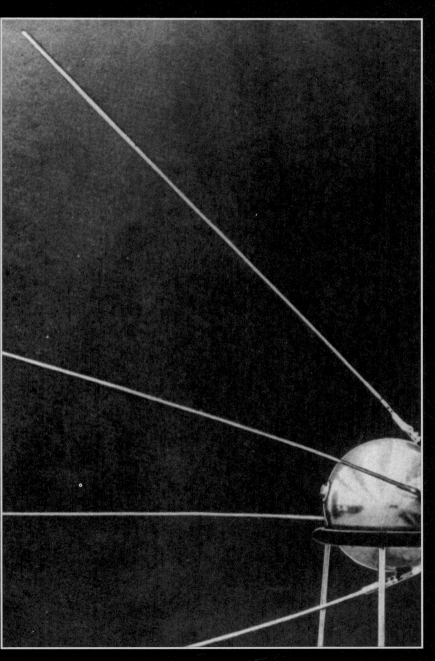

This first official picture of the Soviet satellite *Sputnik I* was
issued in Moscow October 9, 1957, showing the four-antennaed
satellite resting on a three-legged pedestal.

Sputnik II

Von Braun waited hopefully but heard nothing. Then, just about a month after the *Sputnik I* launching, the Soviets put another artificial satellite into orbit. This one was very different from *Sputnik I*. *Sputnik II* was a twelve-foot-long cone, and within it was the first living creature to orbit Earth, a female dog named Laika.

People working on spaceflight knew that the next major step in the "space race" would be to try to put a human being into space. But many wondered if a human being could survive the trip to space. Could a human body stand the terrific acceleration needed to push a satellite out of Earth's atmosphere? Could a human body work as it should in space? A person in space would not have any weight, and would actually float. Could this cause harm? It was necessary to find these things out. A dog's body works very much like a human body, so Soviet scientists had sent a dog into space to find out how it was affected.

Laika Makes Her Fateful Trip

Laika was linked up to devices that sent continuous records of her heartbeat, blood pressure, breathing, and other body functions back to Earth. That enabled the scientists to learn the effects of spaceflight on a creature similar to a human. Laika's cone was heated, air-conditioned, and contained a device that would provide her with meals at regular intervals. A system disposed of her solid and liquid waste. However, there was no way, yet, that a satellite could be brought safely back to Earth. So, after seven days in space, Laika's last meal was to contain a drug to give her a painless death. The Soviets said she had survived for seven days and suffered no ill

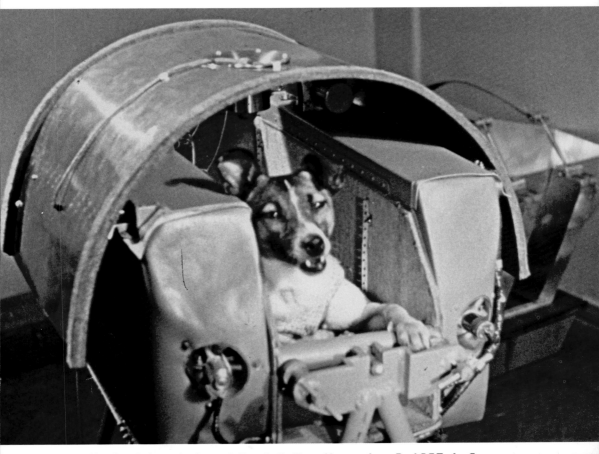

Laika is pictured aboard *Sputnik II* on November 5, 1957, before the Soviets sent her into space.

effects. This seemed to show that humans could be sent into space and survive there. However, in 2002, new evidence revealed that Laika had died from overheating and stress only a few hours after takeoff.[7]

Sputnik I had remained in orbit for three months, but it was gradually pulled lower by Earth's gravity. On January 4, 1958, it entered Earth's atmosphere and was burned up by friction as it fell through the air at tremendous speed.

America Launches Its First Satellite

The U.S. government could no longer ignore what the Soviets were doing. America was losing respect. After *Sputnik II*, the U.S. Army was given permission to attempt a satellite launch, and von Braun and his team sprang into action.

They very quickly produced a satellite that was given the name *Explorer I*. This metal tube resembled a stovepipe with a tapering nose cone. It was six inches wide, about six feet six inches long, and weighed only 30.8 pounds.[8]

The launch took place in secret on January 31, 1958, at Cape Canaveral, Florida. Von Braun's modified Jupiter-C rocket, called *Juno I*, sat waiting, with *Explorer I* inside its nose cone. At 10:48 that night the rocket

The United States launches Juno I, with *Explorer I* inside, at Cape Canaveral, Florida on January 31, 1958.

Explorer 1 Makes an Important Discovery

Explorer 1 reached a height of 1,563 miles above Earth, far higher than either of the Russian satellites.[9] Because it had an instrument aboard to detect radiation, it was able to make a very important scientific discovery. This instrument revealed that there was a belt of high-energy particles with very strong radiation beginning about 600 miles above Earth. This was very important information, because it meant that if human beings did begin going into space, they would have to be protected from radiation. Radiation can do serious harm to a human body, sometimes causing death.

roared up into the sky on a shaft of flame, taking *Explorer I* into space.

The satellite contained equipment for sending electronic signals back to Earth. After eight minutes the signals began and everyone knew the launch was a success. U.S. President Dwight Eisenhower recorded a radio announcement to the world that America had sent a satellite into orbit.

NASA is Created to Provide a "Space Program" for America

It was clear to the world that the Soviet Union and United States were now locked in a competition to explore space and that important new things were being learned. The Soviet Union appeared to be well ahead in the "space race." The Soviets seemed to have a clear plan for what they intended to do in space, but the United States did not seem to have any plan at all. In fact, U.S. President Harry Truman had rejected such a plan.[10] However, in April 1958, the next president, Dwight Eisenhower presented the U.S. Congress with a proposal for a National Aeronautics and Space Agency, an organization to create a "space program" for the United States.

On July 29, 1958, Eisenhower signed the National Aeronautics and Space Act. The next day, he requested from Congress $125 million to start the National Aeronautics and Space Administration (NASA). It was an organization chiefly of groups of scientists and engineers, who would make the plans for what the United States should do in space. The plan they would present would excite the world!

Chapter 3

Now that spacecrafts had successfully been put into space, the next step would be to put people into space.

One of the groups in NASA was known as the Space Task Group. It was responsible for providing a plan for finding out if humans could go into space and survive there. The task group gave their assignment the name Project Mercury, and they went to work.

They decided that first they needed vessels that could take humans into space. Scientists and engineers produced the one-person Mercury capsule. Resembling a bell, it was designed to be carried into space in the nose of an Atlas rocket. The pilot's cabin was in the bell-shaped bottom, and the pilot got into it by going feet-first through a small hatch on the bell's side. Inside the cabin, the pilot strapped himself into a seat. This would reduce the tremendous pressure pushing against his body as the rocket blasted upward at a speed of as much as five miles per second.

Making Spaceflight Safe for the Mercury Pilots

Unlike *Sputnik I*, which had simply been allowed to burn up when it came out of orbit, the Mercury capsule had to be able to bring its human pilot safely back to Earth. It had to have a way of getting out of orbit when the pilot wanted. It had to be able to move down through Earth's atmosphere at tremendous speed without burning up from friction. It had to have a way of making a "soft" landing rather than crashing into the ground.

Using the technology available at that time, scientists and engineers found solutions to these problems. To get out of orbit, the capsule was equipped with what were called retro-rockets. These were a cluster of three small rocket engines called thrusters. They could fire a blast that would slow a capsule in orbit. Once it had slowed enough, gravity would begin pulling the capsule toward Earth. To keep it from burning up as it streaked down through the atmosphere, engineers had invented a "heat shield." This consisted of layers of special plastic on the capsule's bell bottom, which would enter the atmosphere first. The plastic layers would burn away, leaving the metal of the craft undamaged. When the capsule reached a certain altitude, or height above ground, the top section would automatically open and a parachute would snap out. The capsule would then float down to a soft ocean landing.

Selecting the Mercury Project Pilots

Of course, the capsule had to be tested. People would have to be trained to operate it. No human had ever been

The original seven Mercury astronauts were—from left, front row—
Walter Schirra Jr., Donald "Deke" Slayton, John Glenn, and Scott
Carpenter and—from left, back row—Alan Shepard Jr., Virgil "Gus"
Grissom, and Gordon Cooper.

in space, and things that were completely unknown about being in space would have to be discovered. Who could do this?

NASA picked the people who would be trained to fly a Mercury capsule. President Eisenhower made the decision that they should be military test pilots. He believed such men had both the courage and the technical know-how that would be necessary to fly a spacecraft. NASA accepted the president's decision.

America Decides to Go to the Moon

With Project Mercury working on the problem of putting humans into space, NASA held a meeting in December 1958, to discuss what should be the next step. What should America's future goals for spaceflight be?

Wernher von Braun presented a report suggesting that America's goal should be nothing less than to send a man to the Moon. This would be an astounding, earthshaking event and a major American victory in the Cold War. Of course, it was certainly

Very Special People

NASA decided that not just any test pilots could test Mercury capsules. They must have certain special abilities and characteristics. They should have a college degree in either a physical science or engineering, so that they would understand the technology of the vessel they were flying. They should be no more than five feet, eleven inches tall, because a spacecraft would be very cramped, and a taller man would take up too much room. They should be younger than forty, because an older man would probably have less strength and endurance. They should have had at least 1,500 hours of jet flying time, providing them with plenty of experience.

obvious that putting a man on the Moon would be a tremendously difficult, expensive, and perhaps impossible, thing to do. However, von Braun and others felt it could be done within ten years, probably by 1966 or 1967. It was generally agreed that putting an American on the Moon should be NASA's goal.

Project Mercury Gets Underway

Before a manned landing on the Moon could ever be dared, many things would have to be figured out. On October 11, 1958, America launched *Pioneer 1*, one of a series of small spacecraft, designed to gather information about the Moon. These were unmanned spacecraft equipped to take photographs, measure temperature, test for atmosphere, and send all information back to Earth.

In 1959, the Soviet Union began launching its own series of unmanned Moon craft, named Luna, after the scientific name of the Moon. In early 1959, the Soviet *Luna 1* and the U.S. *Pioneer 4* made flights past the Moon, and on September 14, *Luna 2* crashed on the Moon. This was a sensational "first," because it was the first actual "visit" by a spacecraft to another object in space.[1]

Seeing More of the Moon

Less than a month later, the Soviets launched another flight to the Moon, *Luna 3*. At that time the only way to get information about the surface of the Moon was by taking photographs through a telescope. From Earth, it was impossible to get photographs of all parts of the Moon. Because the Moon spins at the same rate as it circles Earth, only one side of the Moon can ever be seen from Earth. In all the thousands of years of human history, no one had ever seen the other side, and it could never be photographed from Earth. But now, *Luna 3*, controlled from Earth, flew around the Moon at a height of forty thousand feet, taking photographs of all parts of the Moon, including the far side, facing away from Earth. These were transmitted back to Earth. It was a time of tremendous excitement for many millions of people, to know they were seeing things that had never been seen before.

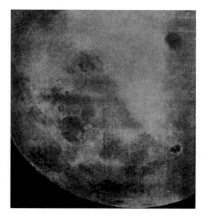

The *Luna 3* spacecraft returned the first views ever of the far side of the moon. The first image was taken on October 7, 1959, at a distance of 39,370 miles after *Luna 3* had passed the Moon and aimed a camera back at the sunlit far side.

Astronauts and Cosmonauts

By January 1959, 110 test pilots of the kind NASA wanted had been accepted to try to become spacecraft pilots. They

The First Monkey Sent Into Space

Before NASA risked any astronauts going into space, it was necessary to make sure they could survive and return safely. Like the Soviet Union, the United States used animals to learn about reactions to acceleration and weightlessness in space. Instead of dogs NASA used monkeys and apes, because these are the animals most like humans. In December 1959, a rhesus monkey named Sam was sent on what was known as a suborbital flight—a flight that went into space, but not far enough to go into orbit. He reached an altitude of fifty-three miles in the nose cone of a V-2-type rocket that brought him safely back to Earth by parachute.

were all men; there were no women test pilots in American military forces at that time. They were tested by doctors and psychologists to check their physical and mental health. By February, the 110 were reduced to 32. These men were then put through many severe tests, such as being spun in circles at tremendous speed in a device called a centrifuge and running on a treadmill until they were exhausted. By April 9, seven pilots had been selected to be the men who would fly the Project Mercury spacecraft. They were given the name "astronauts." This was a word made up from two Greek words, *astron*, meaning star, and *nautes*, meaning sailor. So the word astronaut literally meant, "Star sailor."

Even as the United States was putting together its space program, so was the Soviet Union. Spacecraft were being designed, built, and tested, and men were being trained to operate them. The Soviets called their spacecraft pilots cosmonauts, from Greek words that mean space and sailor.

However, unlike the United States, the Soviet Union was keeping every part of its space program a closely guarded secret.

The First Mercury Spacecraft Test

On July 1, 1960, Wernher von Braun was named director of the NASA Marshall Spaceflight Center in Huntsville, Alabama. The necessary work for Project Mercury had now been completed to the point where testing could begin to see how everything worked. The first test launch of a Mercury capsule into space was made on July 29, 1960. A Mercury capsule was fitted into the nose cone of an Atlas rocket. There was no pilot in the Mercury capsule.

At 9:13 in the morning, the Atlas blasted off in a burst of flame. The sky was overcast and the rocket and its tail of fire quickly disappeared from sight. However, the computer screens keeping track of the Atlas's movement indicated everything was going well.

Then, the screens suddenly went blank. Soon, there was a report from a navy ship in the Atlantic Ocean. At a height of a little more than six miles, traveling at a speed of about fourteen hundred feet per second, the Atlas exploded.[2] Clearly, the Atlas could not do the job. Something else would have to be tried.

Another Failure
and Then Success

After failing to launch a rocket called *Little Joe 5* on November 8, 1960, von Braun and his team decided to try a rocket called the Redstone to which they had made some improvements. A Mercury spacecraft was put onto a Redstone, and in November, the test was made. Again, there was no pilot in the Mercury capsule.

The launch turned into a comedy. A single burst of fire burped from the Redstone's bottom; then there was nothing. The rocket stood silent and motionless.

Von Braun and his engineers were terribly embarrassed, of course, and the newspapers and television comedians made fun of them. However, the cause of the Redstone's behavior was easily found and fixed. Less than a month later on December 19, another test was made with an unmanned Mercury spacecraft on a Redstone rocket. Everything went perfectly.

Project Mercury could continue. The missions that would put men into space could begin. NASA had already made a suborbital flight with a rhesus monkey, but decided one more was needed. With a chimpanzee named Ham, the flight on January 31, 1961, was a complete success.

Most Americans were amused that the first American ventures into space were made by a monkey and an ape, and were delighted that the creatures had returned

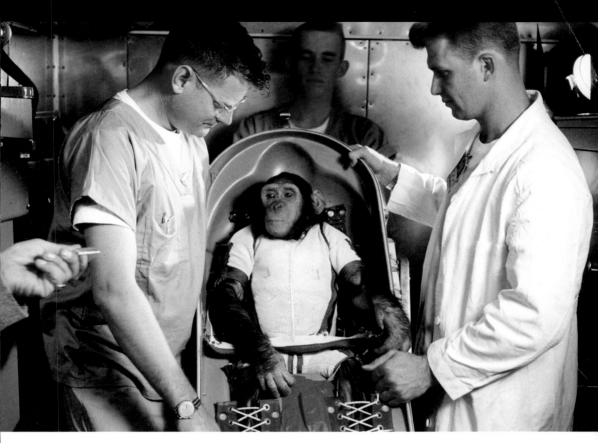

Ham sits in the biopack couch for the MR-2 suborbital test flight. On January 31, 1961, a Mercury-Redstone launch from Cape Canaveral carried the chimpanzee above the Earth.

safely. Americans were fully convinced that the next flight into space would be made by a human.

The First Human Launch Into Space

However, on April 12, 1961, the Soviet Union again thrilled the world and stunned the United States. In southeastern Russia stood a towering metal rocket with a ring of metal cylinders clustered around its lower half. This was known as a multistage rocket—a number of rocket engines connected together. In the nose cone of the giant main rocket was a round metal ball, similar to the one named *Sputnik*. This ball had been named *Vostok 1*, the Russian word for "East." Within the ball, strapped into a padded couch was Russian Air Force pilot Yuri Gagarin. He was wearing a pressure suit and helmet that protected him from extreme cold and extreme heat, and kept him supplied with air.

At 9:07 in the morning, a roaring blast of flame and smoke burst out of the bottom of the giant rocket. Slowly, the rocket began to lift off the ground. Gaining speed, it rose higher and higher, a thick plume of smoke trailing behind it. Soon, it was rushing upward at a speed that kept Gagarin pushed down into his couch as if by a giant invisible hand.

As the craft rose it shed parts of itself. First, the metal sections forming the nose cone came apart and fell clear, exposing the metal ball Gagarin was in. As the fuel in the metal cylinders was used up, they separated from the main rocket and fell back toward Earth. Finally, when the last burst from the main rocket pushed *Vostok 1* out of Earth's upper atmosphere and into space, the main rocket separated and went whirling down.

Now Gagarin's spacecraft, a metal ball with a rocket engine attached, was rushing through space at a speed of nearly eighteen thousand miles per hour, in orbit around Earth.[3] He made one complete orbit, circling the world in one hour and forty-eight minutes.[4] Then, the rocket engine fired a blast that slowed Vostok's speed and gravity pulled it out of orbit and down toward Earth. The engine was automatically separated, and the ball fell toward Earth. The side hitting the atmosphere first was completely covered by a heat shield that kept it from burning up. At twenty thousand feet above the ground, a hatch on the ball opened and Gagarin was automatically ejected through it. A parachute opened above him and he floated safely to the ground.

America Puts Its First Astronaut Into Space

Americans, who had been sure that the first person to go into space would be an American, were shocked, disappointed, and worried by the Soviet triumph.

Twenty-three days after Gagarin's flight, on May 5, 1961, Navy Lieutenant Commander Alan B. Shepard, Jr., became the first American to go into space. He was in a Mercury spacecraft that he had named *Freedom 7*. Like Gagarin, he was strapped in wearing a space suit and helmet. A Redstone rocket carried up the Mercury, but Shepard did not go into orbit as Gagarin did. He made a suborbital flight as Ham the chimpanzee had, reaching an

America's President Makes an Exciting Promise

Although America's first spaceflight was not as spectacular as Gagarin's, it gave pride to many millions of Americans, and renewed confidence in America's space efforts. Then, on May 25, speaking before the U. S. Congress, President John F. Kennedy made a statement that revealed America's plans for future space exploration and excited the world. "I believe that this nation should commit itself to achieving the goal, before this decade is out, of landing a man on the Moon and returning him safely to Earth," he stated. "No single space project in this period will be more exciting, or more impressive to mankind, or more important for the long-range explo-ration of space, and will be so difficult or expensive to accomplish." [7] The President of the United States had just announced that America was going to put all its efforts toward realizing the dream of many people throughout his-tory—a visit to the Moon. Congress broke into a thunder of applause.

altitude of about 117 miles[5] at a top speed of 5,134 miles per hour.[6] Like Ham's craft, Shepard's *Freedom 7* came down in the Atlantic Ocean beneath a parachute.

America Puts Its Second Man Into Space

On July 21, 1961, America sent its second astronaut into space. He was Air Force Captain Virgil I. Grissom, known as "Gus." He had named his spacecraft *Liberty Bell 7*. In it, Grissom reached a height of 118 miles on another suborbital flight, before return-ing to Earth. [8]

Only sixteen days after Grissom's flight, the Soviet Union scored another triumph. Like the Americans, the Soviets were also trying to learn everything they could about the effects of spaceflight on humans. Up to now, only one orbit of a little over an hour and a half had ever been flown by a human, and many people wondered what the effect of several orbits might be. The Soviets made a test to try to find out. On August 6, Soviet cosmonaut Gherman Titov spent more than a full day in space, making seventeen orbits of Earth in a craft called *Vostok 2*. Again, most of the world went wild in praise for the Soviet achievement.

The First American Into Orbit

On November 29, another animal made the first American orbital flight, a chimpanzee named Enos. He went up in a Mercury capsule carried in the nose of an Atlas rocket. But he was brought back after only two orbits when a problem occurred.

Everyone knew that the next American orbital flight would have to be made by a man. On February 20, 1962,

Space-Sickness Appears!

There had been a problem with Titov's flight. For the first five hours everything was fine, but then Titov suddenly began to feel seasick. He became nauseated if he so much as turned his head. His vision became blurry. Finally, Titov simply told the people helping with his flight that he had to sleep. They realized that he was apparently too ill to continue the mission, so they took control of the spacecraft for part of the trip home. However, Titov was well enough to eject from the capsule after re-entry and land by parachute. This was the first case of what became known as space-sickness, from which some other astronauts and cosmonauts would also suffer.

Lieutenant Colonel John H. Glenn, Jr., USMC, became the first American to go into orbit. In a Mercury capsule named *Friendship 7*, he made three, ninety-minute orbits of Earth at a maximum height of 162 miles and speed of 17,500 miles per hour.[9]

In each orbit, Glenn moved from Earth's daylight side, where he could see the planet below through his

John Glenn is pictured inside *Friendship 7*. The capsule was traveling at 17,500 mph.

window, to the night side, where his window showed blackness and brilliant stars. Near the end of the first orbit, when he was coming toward the light, something strange happened. Glenn saw that a cloud of tiny dancing sparks apparently surrounded his spacecraft. By radio, he told the people recording his flight that the ship was " . . . in a big band of some very small particles that are brilliantly lit up like they are luminescent."[10]

As the spacecraft moved out of the darkness into the light, the "particles" vanished. Today, people know that these were tiny ice crystals, shining in the sunlight.

A Terrifying Scare

As Glenn was preparing to come out of orbit, there was a bad moment. Something went wrong with the automatic system controlling *Friendship 7*'s position in space and the craft veered to the right. Using the manual controls, Glenn got the craft back into proper position and held it steady, using his skill as a pilot.

There was another tense moment as Glenn's capsule began to enter Earth's atmosphere. At mission control, a sensor showed that the heat shield of Glenn's craft was no longer locked in place. If that were correct, it would come off as Glenn was going through the atmosphere and his craft would burn up, like a flaming meteor. Fortunately, the sensor was wrong. *Friendship 7* sped through the atmosphere, its parachute flared open, and it dropped safely into the Atlantic Ocean.

John Glenn became America's hero. Newspaper and television reporters loved him, and he was invited to appear on a number of TV talk shows. A song was written about him and recorded by a popular movie star named Walter Brennan. However, NASA still had its larger goal in sight—putting a man on the Moon. Its next set of missions would continue to work toward that achievement.

Chapter 4

In the spring of 1962, NASA called for more test pilots to become astronauts. There were many volunteers, but only nine were accepted. They became known to Americans as "the New Nine." Meanwhile, men who were members of the Mercury Seven were being kept busy on the Mercury Project. On May 24, Navy Lieutenant Commander Scott Carpenter made a three-orbit flight. On October 3, Navy Commander Walter Schirra orbited the Earth six times.

Ideas for Getting to the Moon

The United States had announced its decision to try to land a human being on the Moon, and most people around the world believed the Soviets intended to make a Moon landing. However, compared to what had been done in space so far, a Moon landing was going to be an enormous project. There were tremendous problems to be solved. The first was: Just how was a man, or men, going to be sent to the Moon?

In America there were several ideas for getting to the Moon. One was called Lunar Orbit Rendezvous. Rendezvous is a French word meaning "coming together," so this idea meant coming together in orbit around the Moon. A three-man spacecraft would be launched to the Moon and would go into orbit. It would be carrying a very small, light craft designed to take two men down to the Moon and then back up to the orbiting craft. The orbiting craft would then blast out of orbit and return to Earth. This idea was approved on July 11, 1962.[1]

There were a number of things about flying a spacecraft that would have to be found out before a Moon landing could ever be attempted. One of these was, could two craft in space, moving at thousands of miles per hour, find each other and join together so that astronauts could pass from one craft to another? This would have to be done for a Moon landing. When the little landing craft came back up from the Moon, it would have to attach itself to the orbiting spacecraft so the astronauts could get back inside the spacecraft. First, the landing craft would have to get very close to the orbiting craft, making a rendezvous. Then it would have to attach to the orbiting craft, which was called docking. Could this be done?

In August 1962, the Soviet Union showed that it was working on the docking problem. A spacecraft designated *Vostok 3* was launched into orbit and one day later *Vostok 4* was put into orbit behind it. The two vessels stayed in orbit for several days, and at one point moved to within only four miles of one another. It seemed as if the Soviets were trying to accomplish what was the essential first move for having one ship dock with another in space. However, for the rendezvous to be successful, the ships would have to get much closer.

Project Gemini: A Program for Answering Questions

Docking was not the only thing the United States and Soviet Union had to learn about in order to make a Moon landing. Rocket scientists knew that eventually something was going to happen to one of their orbiting or traveling space vessels that would require a crewman to go outside the vessel to fix it. Medical scientists were not sure this could be done. What would be the effect on a human being of floating in that endless black nothingness without the comfort of a space vessel's walls around him? Might it cause hysteria, unconsciousness, or even some kind of insanity? Might it have some effect on a person's body, such as slowing or speeding the heartbeat?

Still another question was: What difficulties might a long stay in space cause the human body? No astronaut or cosmonaut had spent much more than a day in space. Whoever would go to the Moon would probably spend as much as nine days in space, without gravity, weightless. Would this have any effect on them?

Learning the answers to the questions of docking, living in space, and going outside a ship in space, was the next step for America's space program. NASA's plan was for flights that would practice rendezvous, docking methods, study the effect of long periods in space, and determine the effect of working outside a craft in space. This meant that new kinds of spacecraft and launch vehicles must be designed and built, and crews of astronauts must be trained for each job. In January 1963, Project Gemini began.

Rendezvous Attempts and a "Walk" in Space

Work began on the spacecraft and launchers for Project Gemini. The capsules were slightly larger versions of the Mercury capsule. The Gemini capsule could hold two men. The capsules were equipped with a number of thrusters, small but powerful rocket engines that enabled the craft to turn in different directions and move up or down. The launch rocket for a Gemini capsule would be similar to a Mercury launcher, but larger and with improvements.

On May 15–16, 1963, Air Force Major Gordon Cooper made a twenty-orbit, thirty-four-hour flight in a Mercury capsule called *Faith 7*. The main purpose of the flight was to learn if there might be any effect on a person being in space for more than a day. Since, there was not, Cooper's flight completed the Mercury program.

In June, the Soviets made another rendezvous try. On June 14, 1963, a Vostok spacecraft was launched into orbit, and forty-eight hours later, a second went up. The pilot of the second craft was cosmonaut Valentina Tereshkova, the first woman to go into space. At one point, the two vessels were within three miles of each other.

The Soviets were first to attempt to find out what happened to a human who went outside an orbiting spacecraft. On March 18, 1965, Cosmonauts Pavel Belyayev and Alexei Leonov were launched into orbit in a vessel called *Voskhod 2*, the Russian word for "sunrise." Leonov was the man who would go outside the spacecraft. He was wearing a new type of space suit that was especially made to protect him against the extreme heat and dazzling rays of direct sunlight, which he would be subjected to outside the vessel. Belyayev was also in a space suit, but would remain inside *Voskhod 2*. Both suits had a radio-telephone link built into the helmets, so the two men could talk to each other.

The First "Space Walk"

As soon as *Voskhod 2* was in orbit, Leonov began his mission. He entered a small chamber called an air lock, that could be sealed off from the rest of the spacecraft. On the opposite wall was a round hatch, and after a short interval, he opened it onto the airless void of space. Through this hatch, Leonov would go out into space. There was a sixteen-foot-long, flexible metal tether attached to his spacesuit. The other end of the tether was firmly fastened to the ship, so Leonev would not float away.

Carefully, the cosmonaut put his head and shoulders through the hatchway. Then, he courageously slithered all the way out into space.

Leonev attached a small television camera to the edge of the hatchway. What it showed was recorded back on Earth, and in time, people around the world saw the cosmonaut float out away from the spacecraft until the cord was stretched full length. Then Leonev began to slowly spin at the end of the cord.

Scientists and medical workers had wondered about this moment. Was Leonov having any unpleasant mental or physical experiences? Was he panicking? Was he unconscious?

A Welcome Surprise

As it turned out, Leonov later explained that he was actually enjoying himself as he floated in space. When Belyayev ordered him to return to *Voskhod 2*, Leonov was enjoying himself so much he really did not want to come inside.[2] Thus, the Soviet space walk had shown that humans could safely go outside an orbiting spacecraft, hundreds of miles above Earth, without suffering any mental or physical damage.

However, Leonov was not aware that during the space walk his spacesuit had swollen and become stiff. He was horrified to find that when he tried to re-enter *Voskhod 2*'s air lock he could not bend enough to get through it. Finally, he resorted to lowering the suit's air pressure, which was a serious risk to his body's internal organs. However, this shrank the suit enough so that he was able to pull himself inside.

When the news and television pictures of the first space walk were released, the world went wild. The Soviet Union had now been first to send a spacecraft to another object in space, the Moon; first to put an artificial satellite into orbit; first to put men and a woman into space; and first to send a human outside an orbiting spacecraft! America was lagging badly behind in what was being called the "Space Race."

Five days after Leonov's space walk, the first manned American Gemini flight took place. Designated *Gemini 3*, it was the first American flight of a two-person spacecraft. Astronauts Gus Grissom and John Young flew three orbits during which the craft did some things that no spacecraft had ever done in space before. Using the new Gemini thrusters, pilot Grissom slowed the craft down and then

Edward H. White, II, pilot of the *Gemini 4* spacecraft, floats during the first space walk by an American. In his right hand, White carries a Hand-Held Self-Maneuvering Unit (HHSMU). The visor of his helmet is gold-plated to protect him from the unfiltered rays of the sun.

brought it down into a lower orbit. The mission returned safely to Earth.

Two months later, on June 3, 1965, American astronaut Edward White made the first American space walk from *Gemini 4*. White had an advantage that Leonov did not have. Instead of having to merely pull himself along his lifeline, as Leonov did, White was able to move himself by means of a device that fired bursts of compressed air. This behaved the same way as a rocket engine—shooting a burst of air in one direction pushed White in the opposite direction.

White discovered, as Leonov had, that "walking" in space was enjoyable. "This is fun!" he told his pilot, astronaut James McDivitt.[3] When McDivitt ordered him to return to the spacecraft, White said, "This is the saddest moment of my life."[4]

Like Leonov, White's space suit swelled up slightly and caused him some difficulty in getting back through the air lock. However, the Gemini spacecraft had a better hatch, and McDivitt was able to help pull White through. The entire operation had gone almost perfectly.

A Rendezvous Is Spoiled

Gemini 5 was sent into space on August 21. Its crew was astronaut L. Gordon Cooper and Charles "Pete" Conrad, Jr. The main purpose of the mission was to test the guidance and navigation systems that would be needed to make a rendezvous.

October 25, 1965, was to be America's first attempt at an actual rendezvous. An Atlas booster rocket bearing an Agena spacecraft sat on one launching pad, and half a mile away a Titan Rocket bearing a Gemini spacecraft sat on another. *Gemini 6* held astronauts Wally Schirra and Tom Stafford. The plan was for the Atlas-Agena to be launched into orbit and *Gemini 6* would then go up and try to rendezvous with it.

The Atlas-Agena roared into the sky. It was an excellent launch, but when the Agena separated, its engine blew up! The craft became a cluster of pieces in a cloud of fiery smoke. The second half of the mission had to be called off.

Another Rendezvous Try Goes Wrong

On December 4, the mission was tried again, with some differences. Astronauts Frank Borman and James Lovell were launched in a craft designated *Gemini 7*. It held an extremely large amount of fuel and food supplies, because it was going to stay in orbit for a long time.

Eight days later, on December 12, the second part of the mission began. Wally Schirra and Tom Stafford were again in the cabin of *Gemini 6*, which had been renamed *Gemini 6-A*. They were to be launched into orbit where they would attempt to rendezvous with *Gemini 7*.

The launch nearly became a disaster. At 9:54 in the morning the countdown reached zero, the *Gemini 6-A's* launcher rocket spurted a mountain of smoke and then nothing happened. The engine had suddenly shut down because a plug had come loose. Schirra and Stafford were sitting in the spacecraft atop a launcher with tons of high-explosive rocket fuel that at any moment could blow the rocket, the spacecraft, and the two astronauts to fragments!

Schirra and Stafford sat in the nose cone and waited until the launch crew re-attached the platform, also called a gantry. Then the two astronauts crawled out of their hatches onto the gantry and were taken to safety.

The rendezvous mission was finally accomplished when *Gemini 6-A* was launched on December 15, 1965, to join *Gemini 7*. With both spacecraft moving at a speed of fifteen thousand miles per hour, Schirra, the *Gemini 6-A* pilot, brought the nose of his craft to within twelve inches of the nose of *Gemini 7*.[5] Then he backed off, and for the next four hours, the two vessels remained within twenty feet of one another. The rendezvous was a rousing success.

The mission was also a success in another way. When *Gemini 7* splashed onto the Atlantic Ocean three days

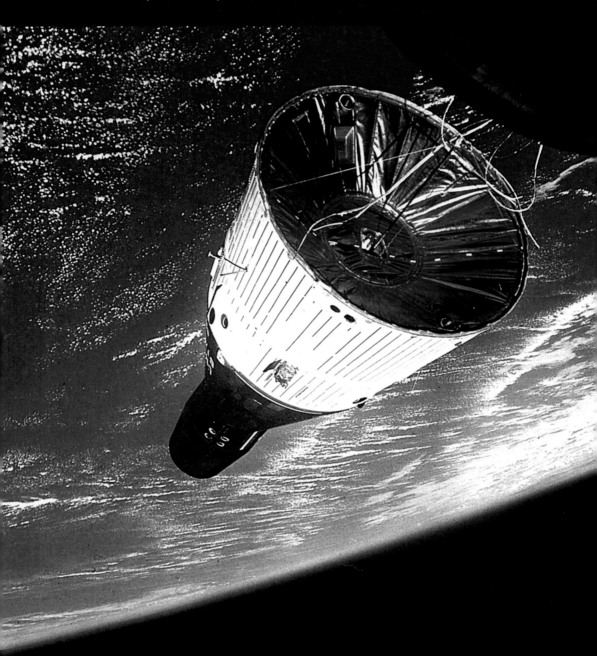

Gemini 7 took this photo of *Gemini 6* during the world's first rendezvous in space, which lasted about five-and-a-half hours at an altitude of 160 miles over the Pacific Ocean.

later, the crew had been in space for fourteen straight days. This answered the question as to whether humans could spend long periods in space without suffering any ill effects. They could.

Docking was still a problem for the people eager for a Moon-landing program. NASA selected March 16, 1966, as the day when another American docking attempt would be made. First, an Agena satellite rocket, specially equipped with a ring inside the flared cone on its tail, was launched into orbit. Then, *Gemini 8*, carrying astronauts Neil Armstrong and David Scott, was launched into the same orbit.

Moving toward the Agena from behind, Armstrong, the Gemini pilot, brought his ship forward a little at a time, using quick bursts of energy from his thrusters. Finally, the Gemini's bottle-shaped nose slid into the Agena's tail cone and was gripped by the ring. The docking was complete, and had been surprisingly easy. Armstrong called it "a smoothie."[6]

However, something had gone wrong. The two locked-together craft began to roll. Armstrong backed his vessel out of the Agena's tail, but the Gemini continued to roll. Fortunately, Armstrong was a skilled pilot, and used the Gemini's orbit-altitude-and-maneuvering system to stop the rolling. He would have to use his skill again as an astronaut in NASA's Apollo program.

Chapter 5

From June 3 to November 11, 1966, there were four more Gemini flights. These were made mainly to practice rendezvous and docking techniques. While the first was cut short because of a mechanical problem, the other missions went perfectly. The problem of docking, one of the major obstacles to a Moon landing, had been solved.

When the last docking test was finished, Project Gemini ended. All its questions and problems had been answered or solved—from the effects of a space walk or a long stay in space on a human, to learning how to rendezvous and dock. Everything was now ready for the beginning of Project Apollo—the project that aimed to land two humans on the Moon.

The Apollo Booster Rocket

Like the Gemini Project, the Apollo Project was designed to be a series of tests leading up to the mission that was the high point of America's space program, landing humans on the Moon. NASA wanted to make sure that everything that needed to be known had been learned and that everything would work as it was supposed to. Most of these tests, or missions, would be made by crews of astronauts, flying in Apollo spacecraft.

For years, thousands of scientists and engineers had been designing, planning, and putting together the craft that would take humans to the Moon. By early 1966, Wernher von Braun and his team had produced a gigantic booster rocket called Saturn V. It towered more than 363 feet high,[1] taller than the Statue of Liberty,[2] and it consisted of three parts or "stages." The first stage, at the bottom, had five engines that would drive the craft up to a height of forty-two miles at a speed of six thousand miles per hour.[3] At that point, the first stage would separate from the rest of the booster. The second stage, consisting of the middle part of the booster and its engines, would then kick the craft up to 115 miles and separate. Finally, the third stage, the top portion of the booster, would speed up

Project Apollo Gets a Chief of Flight Crew Operations

One of the first seven astronauts picked for the Mercury program was Donald Slayton, nicknamed Deke. He had been a bomber pilot during World War II, and after the war worked as an aeronautical engineer. In 1962, as an astronaut, he was assigned to become the second American to go into orbit. However, two weeks before he was due to make his flight, doctors discovered he had developed heart problems. His flight into space was cancelled, and he was forbidden to ever fly again, even in an airplane.

Slayton was too useful and competent a person to be put on the shelf. When Project Apollo began, he received the position of chief of flight crew operations, which meant that he would select the spacecraft crew for each Apollo mission.

HEIGHT = 363 FT.
APOLLO / SATURN V
SPACE VEHICLE

HEIGHT = 305 FT.
STATUE OF
LIBERTY

MSFC 67 PA 117

This 1967 illustration compares the Apollo Saturn V spacecraft of the Moon-landing era to the Statue of Liberty located on Ellis Island in New York City. The Apollo Saturn V, at 363 feet, towers above the Statue of Liberty, standing at 305 feet.

to twenty-five thousand miles per hour. This is what is known as "escape velocity," the speed necessary to break free of Earth's gravity and "escape" into outer space.

The Three-Piece Apollo Spacecraft

The Saturn V was designed to carry three small space-craft into space—a command module, a service module, and a Moon-landing vehicle. The command module (CM) was a ten-and-one-half foot-high cone that carried the three-man crew and the instruments for controlling the module and for communicating by radio. The service module (SM) was a twenty-three-foot-long cylinder that contained an electrical-supply unit, fuel tanks, and a rocket engine.

The Moon-landing vehicle was the spacecraft that would carry two men and land on the Moon. This lunar module (LM), was just two compartments, one on top of the other. The top compartment was round with bulges on its sides and a square hatch on its front. It contained the cabin, which the two astronauts would be inside as the LM dropped toward the Moon's surface. The bottom compartment was an octagon shape. Slim tubular legs jutted out of four of the eight sides, to provide landing gear. The LM was about twenty-three feet high and fourteen feet wide.

When a Saturn V was launched, the CM with the SM attached behind it were carried at the top of the Saturn launch vehicle. Attached this way, they were known as a command/service module (CSM). Behind them, inside the launch vehicle, was the LM.

When the third stage of the booster rocket reached escape velocity, the CSM and the LM would be put together, or docked. Shortly after this, the third stage of the booster would fall away. The CSM and LM, now forming a single craft, would continue on, straight for the Moon. All these steps and operations were how the people working on Project Apollo believed the flight to the Moon would be made. But every step of the operation had to be tested and, in some cases, retested.

A Test That Became a Tragedy

The first official "mission" of Project Apollo was supposed to be a test of what would become *Apollo 1*, the first of the kind of spacecraft that would land humans on the Moon. In the top of a Saturn IB booster rocket on the launchpad, was an Apollo CSM. It was filled with pure oxygen for the astronauts to breathe, as in a real launch. Everything would be checked to see how it worked. No one expected any problems.

A little before one o'clock on the afternoon of January 27, 1967, three astronauts in space suits squirmed through the module's hatch. The three men were Gus Grissom, Edward White, and Roger Chaffee. They represented a typical three-man crew of an Apollo spacecraft. They strapped themselves into the craft's padded couches.

The crew inside the spacecraft and the launch pad technicians outside waited in boredom as various "glitches" held things up. Then, suddenly, the people in communication with the spacecraft heard Roger Chaffee's

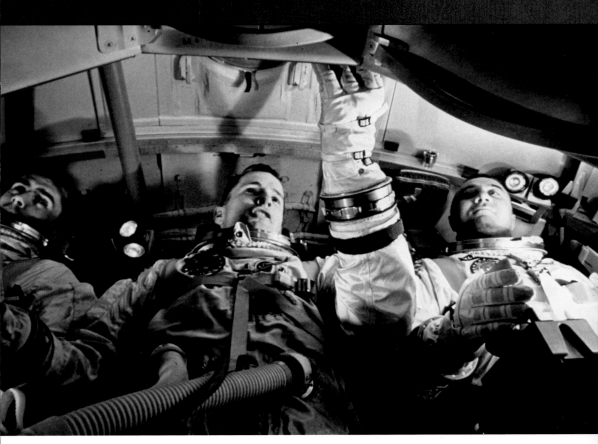

The prime crew of the *Apollo I* spacecraft go through a practice session on January 1967. The astronauts Roger Chaffee (left), Edward H. White, II (center), and Virgil Grissom were killed during another testing session on January 27, at Cape Kennedy, Florida, when a flash fire swept their cabin.

voice shout over the radio, "We've got a fire in the cockpit!"[3] There was a fire inside the craft.

Horrified men outside could see through the window that there were flames blazing inside the cabin. "Blow the hatch!" someone yelled, meaning that someone should make use of the explosive device that could blow the hatch open from outside. Inside, Grissom and White, engulfed in flames were struggling to open the hatch, but

The Soviets Also Suffer a Setback

The Soviets had developed a new type of spacecraft they named Soyuz ("Union"), which, like the American Apollo, was designed to carry a landing craft to the Moon. With this vessel, the Soviet Union was even with America in the race to be first to put a man on the Moon.

Soyuz's first test was set for April 23, 1967. The launch was satisfactory and the craft went into orbit, but when the pilot, Vladimir Komarov, tried to land, the parachute failed. *Soyuz 1* smashed into the ground at hundreds of miles per hour and Komarov became the first person to die during a spaceflight. This tragedy was a setback to the Soviet space program.

it was held in place by bolts that had to be unscrewed. All the men on the gantry were rushing to the module, but it was hopeless.

Investigators later determined that the tragedy was caused by a short circuit in the electrical wiring in the command module. A glowing spark from the short ignited the pure oxygen, which burns very quickly. Fire exploded through the module. The last thing heard from the crew were screams of pain. All three astronauts died. The module was badly damaged.

Why had the *Apollo 1* disaster happened? NASA began an immediate investigation with hundreds of people testing, probing, studying, and searching for mistakes and mechanical failures. What they found was shocking. What had caused the explosive fire was now easy to see, but no one had noticed before. The *Apollo 1* command module had been crammed with flammable materials, such as foam plastic couch padding and plastic netting. The 100-percent oxygen that filled the module literally turned it into a bomb ready to explode. No one had considered any of this. The project was put on hold, while everything about the Apollo command module was reexamined, re-thought, and re-designed.

Testing the Mighty Saturn V Booster

After some nine months of intense work on virtually redesigning the Apollo command module, NASA scheduled the second Apollo mission on November 9, 1967. It was to be a test to see if the problems that had destroyed *Apollo 1* had been solved and if an Apollo spacecraft could be put into orbit. An Apollo command module had been put into the nose cone of a Saturn V booster rocket that would carry it into space. This was the first actual launch of a Saturn V rocket and the mission was officially designated *Apollo 4*. There was no crew in the command module because NASA was fearful of losing any more men if something went wrong.

The countdown proceeded to zero. For the crowds watching the launch at Cape Kennedy from a distance, the ground actually seemed to begin shaking as an eruption of swirling white flame and yellow smoke poured out of the five giant engines at the bottom of the booster and spread in all directions.[4] The Saturn seemed to be poised

The *Apollo 4* unmanned mission lifts off from launch pad 39A at the Kennedy Space Center. This would be the first flight of the enormous Saturn V rocket that would eventually take humans to the Moon.

on a lake of fire and steam. Then, gradually, it began to creep upward. Suddenly, a shocking roar of noise hammered the watching crowd of thousands. The booster moved faster, thrusting upward. Its speed increased until it vanished into the sky.

At thirty-eight miles above Earth, the first stage shut down and separated. The second stage engines ignited, and continued to push the rocket upward. The second stage next shut down, and it fell away. The third stage's huge engine ignited and carried the command module into orbit. It had been a perfect launch!

More Tests With Mixed Results

Launched on January 22, 1968, *Apollo 5* was another unmanned mission. Its basic purpose was to test how a lunar module performed in actual spaceflight. Tests of the LM on Earth had not always been satisfactory, but those tests were made in air and gravity. How would things work in airless, weightless space?

The LM was carried into orbit by another Saturn V booster. Everything was checked out by means of automatic processes controlled from Earth. The results were found to be satisfactory.

Apollo 6 was essentially a re-do of *Apollo 4*—a test of the launch of a Saturn V booster. Would the giant rocket perform as well as it had previously?

The Soviets Threaten to Pull Ahead

Nothing much had been heard from the Soviet space program since the tragic death of cosmonaut Komarov and destruction of *Soyuz 1* in April 1967. On the afternoon of October 25, NASA learned that there had been a launch of a large Soyuz-type spacecraft in Kazakhstan. The next day, Soviet authorities announced that a cosmonaut piloting a *Soyuz 3* had a rendezvoused with an unmanned *Soyuz 2*, launched the day before. Both craft performed well and were brought down safely. Clearly, the Soviet space program was back on track, in competition with the Apollo Project. Many people around the world believed that the Soviets might try making a manned flight around the Moon as soon as December. This would put the Soviet Union ahead in the "Moon race."

The answer turned out to be no. Several things went badly wrong. The booster began to bounce as it rose. When the second-stage engines ignited, one of them suddenly went dead. When the third-stage engine was supposed to reignite for escape velocity, it did not do so. The Saturn was simply stuck in orbit. Wernher von Braun and his engineers rushed back to their workplace to try to figure out what had gone wrong, which they determined in only twenty days. They assured NASA that the next Apollo launch would work flawlessly. Project Apollo was back on schedule.

The next Apollo mission, designated *Apollo 7*, was the first Apollo flight with a crew in place. The crew was Walter M. Schirra, commander, Donn F. Eisele, and R. Walter

Cunningham. The mission's purpose was to test the Apollo CSM, the linked-together command module and service module. This was a very complicated spacecraft, with a lot of connected parts that all needed to work perfectly to avoid trouble, and the NASA engineers were worried. They expected problems—they just could not guess which problems.

The CSM was carried into orbit by a Saturn IB booster rocket on October 11, 1968, and stayed in orbit for nearly eleven days. Nothing went wrong, and the mission was considered a complete success.

Chapter 6

For some time, NASA believed that *Apollo 8* should be an actual manned flight to the Moon—everything but a landing. The activities of the Soviet space program now made NASA decide that a manned spaceflight to the Moon should indeed be America's next move. On December 21, 1968, with a crew consisting of Frank Borman, commander; James Lovell; and William Anders, *Apollo 8* was launched on a Saturn V booster in a fountain of white flame. Eleven-and-a-half minutes later, Saturn's first and second stages were gone and *Apollo 8*, consisting of only a command module (CM) and service module (SM) with no lunar module (LM), was in orbit. Some two hours and thirty-six minutes after that, the third stage automatically roared into life and began to increase the speed to the twenty-five-thousand-mile-per-hour escape velocity. *Apollo 8* was on its way to the Moon, the first spacecraft to bring men there from Earth. In its cabin, the astronauts heard an excited voice from Mission Control: "You're on your way! You're *really* on your way!" [1]

Looking the Moon Over

Some time after *Apollo 8* was launched, Deke Slayton, chief of flight crew operations for the Apollo Program, called astronaut Neil Armstrong into his office. Armstrong had been a Navy Panther jet attack pilot on the aircraft carrier *Essex*. He had flown seventy-eight combat missions. He had also participated in some of the Gemini missions. Slayton asked him if he wanted to be the commander of *Apollo 11*. This might be the mission that would land two men on the Moon. Armstrong told him that he would accept command.

This is how the Earth looked as photographed from a point near the Moon by the *Apollo 8* astronauts.

As *Apollo 8* sped toward the Moon, it was necessary to slowly rotate the craft in order to keep the temperature on the hull even. If sunlight fell on only one side of the craft, it would overheat. Borman, in command, was rotating it about one full turn every hour. For a short time during each rotation, Earth was visible out of one of the windows, a blue and white ball. Each time it seemed a little smaller. The crew of *Apollo 8* were moving farther away from Earth than any human had ever been. In time, Earth was small enough to be covered by an astronaut's thumb.[2]

Apollo 8 continued to move closer to the Moon. Soon Borman would flip the switch that would cause the service module engine to ignite, slowing the speeding spacecraft down and putting *Apollo 8* into orbit around the Moon. Just about three minutes before he got the signal to do so, the spacecraft sailed over the daylight side of the Moon. The Moon became visible to the astronauts. What they saw, from a height of sixty-nine miles above the surface, was a vast gray expanse covered with craters of every possible size. Flat areas were speckled with tiny craters within small craters, within larger craters. The sides of mountains were dotted with craters. For billions of years, meteoroids, moving pieces of rock and metal of all sizes, had been streaking down out of space and crashing onto the Moon's surface. This was the result— a surface speckled with millions of different-sized craters.

The crew of *Apollo 8* would not land on the Moon, but they were the first humans to ever see it this close.

Preparing for the Last Two Test Missions

When the time came, Borman placed *Apollo 8* into orbit. It began the first of the ten orbits it would make around the Moon, the first manned Earth spacecraft to ever orbit the Moon. Back on Earth, it was Christmas Eve.

During their orbits of the Moon, the astronauts took many photographs that would help determine where the Moon landing would be made. At what was nineteen minutes after midnight on Christmas Day, the service module engine fired to take *Apollo 8* out of orbit. Moments later, it began its return trip to Earth. Three days later, on the morning of December 27, 1968, it splashed down in the Pacific Ocean.

Two more missions were scheduled before the possible Moon-landing mission, and the purpose of both was to make critical tests of the LM. Everything depended on that awkward, flimsy craft. It had to successfully undock from the command module, fly down to the Moon, and land safely. Then, to return the astronauts safely, it had to separate into two parts, and the top part had to successfully fly back up and re-dock with the command module. Any number of things might go wrong. If an engine failed,

The *Apollo 11* Crew

On the morning of January 6, 1969, Deke Slayton called Neil Armstrong, and astronauts Edwin "Buzz" Aldrin and Michael Collins, into his office. Aldrin had been an Air Force fighter pilot during the Korean War, and Collins had been a test pilot before coming to NASA. Armstrong, Collins, and Aldrin all knew one another quite well. Slayton informed them that if missions 9 and 10 were both successful, Mission 11 would be the craft that would go to the Moon and land two men on it. Armstrong, Collins, and Aldrin would be its crew, with Armstrong, the commander; Collins, the command module pilot; and Aldrin, the LM pilot. The three men were excited. Almost at once they began training for the mission. Michael Collins, who was to be the pilot, spent nearly all his time thoroughly mastering the CSM controls. Armstrong and Aldrin, who would be the two men going down and coming back up in the LM began thoroughly checking its computers. They had to try to anticipate difficulties. "What are we going to do if this happens," they would ask one another, speaking of some possible unexpected event. They would then test and experiment until they found out what they could do to prevent it.

if a mechanical part did not work properly, if the LM's radar went wrong, the two astronauts could be killed in a crash, stranded on the Moon, or marooned in space to die when their oxygen ran out. To prevent any such thing from happening, the two test missions, called *Apollo 9* and *Apollo 10*, were scheduled.

Apollo 9 was launched on March 3, 1969. The crew was James McDivitt; commander; David Scott; and Russell Schweickart. The huge Saturn launch rocket roared up on a fountain of flame. The third stage flared and fell away. The second stage carried its load into orbit and fell away.

The CSM was attached to the third stage of the Saturn rocket by bolts that had explosive charges built into their heads. The flick of a switch on the command module would blow the bolt heads off and enable the CSM, called *Gumdrop*, to float free of the third stage. Scott, the command module pilot, flicked the switch.

The CSM was now free of the third stage, but the LM, called *Spider*, was still inside it. Scott fired some thrusters that turned and rotated *Gumdrop* so it could approach the LM nose first. He then eased *Gumdrop* forward until its docking nose slid into the ring on the LM's roof. The LM, the command module, and the service module were now all linked together in order. *Apollo 9* was now complete. The third stage of the booster was drifting away beneath it.

The First LM Test Is Successful

The docking process automatically provided an airtight "tunnel" connecting the LM and command module. Following the crew's sleep period, McDivitt and Schweickart began putting on their space suits to go through the tunnel into the LM. However, they both now suddenly began to experience the dizziness and nausea of space-sickness. This was a serious matter, because if a man wearing space helmet began to throw up, he could choke on his own vomit. Fortunately, both men soon recovered and were able to continue into the LM. The tests began.

Gumdrop and Spider

After the third stage of the Saturn carried the CSM and LM into orbit during *Apollo 9*, they would be set free and the tests would begin. For much of the time the CSM and the LM would then be separated. They would be sending and receiving messages to and from Earth and each other, and it would be necessary to know which vehicle a message was meant for or coming from. Thus, each vehicle had to have a distinct name during the time they were separated. The name that had been chosen for the CSM was *Gumdrop*, because of its conical shape. The LM was called *Spider*, because of its bulky "body" and long, thin legs.

By the fifth day of the ten-day mission, the LM crew had undocked *Spider* from *Gumdrop*, flown the LM 111 miles from the command module and back, and re-docked with it.[3] They had done everything the LM would have to do on the Moon landing mission. Schweickart had also gone outside the LM to make a thirty-eight minute test of the space suit and life-support backpack that would be worn by the men who landed on the Moon. However, during all this time, both men suffered from occasional attacks of space-sickness or, at any rate, nausea. Despite this, *Apollo 9* was considered a success.

There was now only one more test before the actual Moon landing flight was to take place. This test would be like what actors call a dress rehearsal for a play. That is when everyone is in costume and the play is put on exactly as it will be before a huge audience on opening night. It is a way of making sure everything will go exactly as it should. The dress

The *Apollo 9* lunar module was named *Spider.*

rehearsal for the Moon landing was to be an actual flight to the Moon and back, with a simulated, or imitation, Moon landing by the LM, to make sure that an Apollo spacecraft could actually do everything it was supposed to do.

The spacecraft making the flight was *Apollo 10.* Its crew was Thomas Stafford, commander, and astronauts Eugene Cernan and John Young. The launch was on May 18, 1969. Again, for the crowds of people watching the launch at Cape Kennedy, Florida, the ground

Apollo 9 Command/Service Modules (CSM), named *Gumdrop*, and Lunar Module (LM), named *Spider*, are shown docked together as Command Module pilot David R. Scott stands in the open hatch.

actually seemed to be shaking as the enormous Saturn V booster rocket lifted off out of the eruption of spreading, swirling smoke.

As with the previous mission, the command module and LM were given names for use while they were being operated separately. The command module would be *Charlie Brown*, the central character in the popular comic strip "Peanuts." The LM was named *Snoopy*, after Charlie Brown's dog. When the third stage of the Saturn fired to speed up to escape velocity, *Charlie Brown*'s pilot, John Young, used his craft's thrusters to turn it end over end, and docked with *Snoopy*. The third stage fell away and *Apollo 10*, linked together as a single vehicle, proceeded to the Moon.

The Second LM Test Begins

At the end of the three-day journey, the engine was fired, putting the spacecraft into orbit. The next day, Stafford and Cernan entered the LM and John Young undocked the modules, pulling *Charlie Brown* free of *Snoopy*. In the LM, Tom Stafford punched a command into the computer. *Snoopy* began to drop toward the Moon.

Snoopy would not land on the Moon, but would fly close to the surfaces, then back up, simulating an actual Moon landing. There was a rocket engine in the LM's bottom portion and another in the top portion. It was the engine in the bottom, called the descent engine that would enable the LM to fly down. It would be descending toward the Moon, at a speed of nearly thirty-seven hundred miles per hour. By firing a steady burst of energy from the descent engine along the flight direction, Snoopy would be slowed down to a steady descent.[4]

Snoopy Shows How It Should Be Done

The engine in the top portion was known as the ascent engine. Bursts of energy from it, pushing down, would thrust the LM up to where it could rejoin the command module. What Stafford and Cernan were now doing was testing all these things, to make sure they worked properly.

When the LM actually landed on the Moon during the next mission, only the top part of it would leave. The bottom portion of the LM was constructed to become a launching pad from which the top portion, with the two astronauts inside, would take off to rejoin the CSM in orbit. Thus, for this simulation of a Moon landing, the bottom part of Snoopy would be detached to fall onto the Moon.

At forty-seven thousand feet above the Moon's surface, Stafford turned Snoopy around.[5] Suddenly, the LM began to swing rapidly from left to right causing Cernan to give a shout of dismay that startled the men listening at Mission Control.[6] There was danger that *Snoopy* might go out of control and crash. What had happened was that a switch had somehow been jiggled into the wrong position and the LM's computer was trying to set things right. This was exactly the sort of problem the test was supposed to find. Stafford quickly switched to manual control, and Snoopy's wild movements stopped. The LM's bottom part was dropped off, and the ascent engine began taking the top upward. At about seventy thousand feet, *Snoopy* redocked with *Charlie Brown*, and Stafford and Cernan rejoined Young in the command module. *Snoopy* was cut loose and the command module was

The Soviet Union Is Forced Out of the Moon Race

By summer 1969, the Soviet Union had reluctantly decided that America would win "the race" to the Moon. However, the Soviets had not given up entirely. They were working hard to be second to put men on the Moon. There was also the possibility that if the American Moon landing attempt should fail, the Soviets could still arrive first.

Therefore, NASA was watching anxiously as the Soviets appeared to be readying a double launch of a manned Moon landing test flight in early July. On the morning of July 4, an American spy satellite passing overhead photographed a fueling operation at one of the huge Soviet boosters.

However, when the American satellite passed over the site in the late afternoon, photographs showed a scene of horrifying destruction. The booster that had been fueled was gone, the machines that had stood around it were gone, the entire area for several miles around was scorched and blackened. Clearly, there had been a tremendous fuel explosion, and the Soviet launch had been destroyed. The Soviet Union was out of the Moon race.

From left to right, Commander Neil A. Armstrong, Command Module Pilot Michael Collins, and Lunar Module Pilot Edwin "Buzz" Aldrin, Jr., were the crew of the *Apollo 11.*

ready for return to Earth. Except for a jiggled switch, the mission had been perfect. The next mission might be the one to put men on the Moon

At a meeting in March, attended by astronauts and a number of NASA officials, a major decision was reached. It was decided that on July 16, *Apollo 11* would be launched to the Moon. Everyone now knew where things stood.

Chapter 7

Work continued on the American Moon-landing mission, *Apollo 11*. What had not been determined was who would be the first man to step onto the Moon? Whoever it was would become one of the most famous people in all history. Probably most of the astronauts wished they could be the one. Buzz Aldrin had been thinking about this. Only he and Neil Armstrong would be on the Moon. Only one of them could be the one to make history.

Aldrin may have felt he had a good chance. During the Gemini Program space walks, there was an order that the commander always stayed inside the spacecraft and never went outside. Later, when LM's were being tested, the LM pilot was considered first in line to leave the ship and make the test. Aldrin was the LM pilot for *Apollo 11*. Did that mean he was supposed to be the one to leave the ship first? He knew that an earlier plan for *Apollo 11* had specified that, but it had never been verified.

Aldrin apparently decided to talk to Armstrong about what was to happen. He urged that they needed to come to a decision, and frankly admitted that he would like to be first to step onto the Moon. Armstrong answered that he fully understood the historical significance of being first on the Moon and did not want rule himself out.

Commander Neil Armstrong was picked to be the first man to walk on the Moon.

Aldrin went to a NASA official to urge that a decision be made. A few days later, Deke Slayton met with Aldrin and Armstrong. He informed them that a decision had been made—Armstrong would be the first man to leave the LM and step onto the Moon. There were good reasons for this. Armstrong would be seated next to the hatch and it would be far easier for him to open it and slide himself out, than for Aldrin to squeeze past him in the tiny cramped cabin with the bulky space suit and huge life-support backpack he would be wearing. Also, Slayton told Aldrin that Armstrong deserved to be first man on the Moon because of his position as the mission commander.

Apollo 11 in Danger?

On July 13, 1969, three days before *Apollo 11* was due to be launched, NASA received information that caused fear among all the people

Choosing Names

Because this was the mission that would be one of the greatest events of human history, NASA felt that everything about it had to be dead serious and on a high level. Thus, giving the command module and LM names such as *Gumdrop* and *Snoopy* simply would not do. The three astronauts and their wives had actually spent several months trying to think up suitable names that would appeal to the American people. The names that Armstrong, Aldrin, and Collins finally settled on were *Columbia* for the command ship and *Eagle* for the lunar module. Columbia is another name for the United States, after Christopher Columbus, and the Bald Eagle is the national bird of America.

working on the *Apollo 11* mission. They learned that the Soviet Union had sent a large robot-controlled rocket to the Moon. Apparently, the Soviet craft was supposed to crash-land on the Moon, scoop up Moon rocks and soil, and bring them back to Earth in a small robot craft contained inside the big one. Perhaps the Soviets felt this would let them share in America's triumph of landing on the Moon.

Some Americans feared that the Russian craft might damage the American LM that would be on the Moon, or might even affect the movement of the American command module that would be in orbit around the Moon, although this would have been almost impossible. However, to ensure that nothing could happen, the Soviet Union sent full information showing that the Soviet craft would not be any threat.

The crew of the *Apollo 11* was ready to make history.

Liftoff

55 seconds and counting. Neil Armstrong just reported back. It's been a real smooth countdown. We have passed the 50-second mark. Our transfer is complete on an internal power with the launch vehicle at this time.
40 seconds away from the Apollo 11 *liftoff.*
All the second stage tanks now pressurized.

35 seconds and counting. We are still go with
Apollo 11.
30 seconds and counting. Astronauts reported,
feels good.
T-25 seconds.
20 seconds and counting.
T-15 seconds, guidance is internal,
12,
11,
10,
9, ignition sequence starts,
6,
5,
4,
3,
2,
1,
zero, all engines running,
LIFTOFF.
We have a liftoff, 32 minutes past the hour.
Liftoff on Apollo 11.[1]

These words from Mission Control announced liftoff
of the huge Saturn V carrying *Apollo 11* at 9:32 on the
morning of July 16, 1969. The crowd again experienced
the shaking of the ground and the onslaught of incredible
noise as the booster rose into the sky. About two hours

A plume of flame signals the liftoff of the *Apollo 11* Saturn V space vehicle and astronauts Neil Armstrong, Michael Collins, and Edwin "Buzz" Aldrin, Jr., from Kennedy Space Center.

and forty-five minutes later, Collins was beginning the docking procedure, fastening the CSM to the LM.

On July 20, 1969, *Apollo 11* was going into orbit around the Moon. There was a continuous amount of "housework" to be done by the astronauts. Batteries had to be re-charged. Water had to be chlorinated to keep it drinkable. Wastewater had to be dumped.

As *Apollo 11* was slowing down to go into orbit, the Columbia pilot, Michael Collins, decided to treat everyone who could hear him on Earth to a description of the kind of food astronauts ate. He assured his listeners that there was plenty of coffee, fruit beverages, and small bites of bacon. He described how, by simply adding water, a beautiful chicken stew could be produced. He was lavish in his praise of the NASA chef's salmon salad.

Eight Miles Above the Moon

As *Apollo 11* orbited over the Moon, Armstrong and Aldrin floated through the tunnel between the CM *Columbia* and the LM *Eagle*. They stood side by side, attached to the floor of the LM by elastic cords, staring at the numbers blinking on the computer screen "You are go for separation, *Columbia*," said the voice of the man at Houston in radio communication with *Apollo 11*.[2]

Collins pressed the button that operated the docking mechanism, separating *Columbia* from the LM. As the two vehicles moved apart, the two men on *Eagle* heard Collins tell them, "Okay, *Eagle*, you guys take care."[3]

The *Eagle* was flying with its bottom and descent engine pointed in the flight direction. Aldrin flipped the switch that fired the descent engine and began to drop

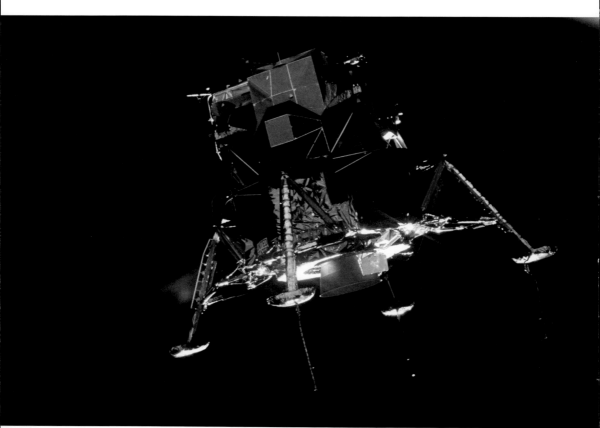

The *Apollo 11* lunar module *Eagle* was photographed in lunar orbit from *Columbia* as the *Eagle* gets into landing position. The long rod-like objects under the landing pods are lunar-surface-sensing probes. Upon contact with the lunar surface, the probes send a signal to the crew to shut down the descent engine.

down to eight miles above the surface. When it reached that point, Mission Control in Houston would tell the two astronauts if they could land or if they would have to end the landing attempt and return to *Columbia*. That would mean the mission was a failure.

"*Eagle*, Houston," said the voice on the radio. "You're a GO for powered descent."[4]

Aldrin and Armstrong grinned at each other. They were going to land on the Moon!

Suddenly, the number 1202 began to flash on *Eagle's* computer. This was bad news. It meant that the LM's computer was overloaded. It could also mean that something was wrong with the computer and the landing should be called off. Anxiously, Neil Armstrong checked with Mission Control, and the problem was resolved.

"You're go for landing," said Mission Control.[5]

The landing was still on. However, *Eagle* was now less than one thousand feet above the surface, which did not look good to Armstrong. The computer seemed to be taking the LM down into a field of boulders. This was a tremendously dangerous situation. If they landed in a place where the ground was uneven, *Eagle* could topple over. Even if Armstrong and Aldrin were not injured, they would be doomed. *Eagle* would not be able to take off and the two men could stay alive only as long as their oxygen lasted. The entire mission would be a failure and two lives would be lost.

The Landing on the Moon

Armstrong was not willing to risk landing where *Eagle* was headed. He took over manual control of the LM and changed its descent so it would pass over the boulders. It was now two hundred feet above the surface and descending less than three feet a second. The descent engine was almost out of fuel. Armstrong fired a long, steady burst.

The *Eagle* came down so gently that neither Armstrong nor Aldrin was aware the landing had been made. However, a blue light with the words "Lunar Contact" beneath it was glowing on the instrument panel. This meant that the LM was on the Moon. Armstrong reached out and pressed a button marked "Engine Stop." "Shutdown," he said.

At Mission Control, many of the men were holding their breath, their faces showing expressions of concern. They knew that *Eagle* was nearly out of fuel. What was happening? Had the landing been made? Were the astronauts safe?

Then, suddenly, they heard Neil Armstrong's voice. "Houston, Tranquility base here," he said. "The *Eagle* has landed."[6] The *Eagle* had landed in a region of the Moon known as the Sea of Tranquility.

Preparing for a Moon Walk

At Mission Control the tension vanished. "You've got a bunch of guys about to turn blue!" the man communicating with them told Armstrong. "We're breathing again. Thanks a lot."[7] On the Moon, Aldrin reached out and firmly shook Armstrong's hand.

The two astronauts were now supposed to eat a light meal and sleep, but they were simply too excited. Through the LM window they could see that they had come down in a relatively flat area that was covered with craters that looked to be from as much as one hundred feet wide down to less than a foot. There were far more small ones than large ones, and the area between them was packed with rocks of all sizes and shapes. Off to one side was a cluster of boulders that seemed to range in size from one to two feet.

The two astronauts were wild with excitement to get out among these craters and rocks, and they began getting ready for their "Moon walk." Actually, most astronauts did not use the term "Moon walk," especially when they were talking to each other on the radio. They used the official NASA term EVA, which stood for Extra-Vehicular Activity—doing things outside the vehicle. Thus, when Armstrong and Aldrin were later on the Moon, *Columbia*'s pilot, Mike Collins, talking to astronaut Bruce McCandless who was acting as capsule communicator at Mission Control, asked how the EVA was going. McCandless replied, "beautifully."[8]

Before they stepped on the Moon, however, Armstrong and Aldrin began putting on their EVA pressurized suits, helmets, and life-support backpacks. This took a long time. The backpack was twenty-six inches long, a little less than eighteen inches wide, and ten and one-half inches deep. It was literally packed with things that would keep its wearer alive on the Moon—an oxygen-supply system that automatically pumped air into the space suit, and a system that kept the air moving through the entire suit, and a cooling system that would keep the suit from overheating. On top of the backpack was a thirty-minute emergency supply of oxygen in case something went wrong with the main supply. Together, the space suit and emergency pack weighed about 190 pounds on Earth, but their combined weight in the Moon's gravity was only about 30 pounds.[9]

Finally, the astronauts opened the hatch on *Eagle*'s front. Armstrong, as the mission's commander, was the man who would go out first. "Okay, About ready to go down and get some Moon rock?"[10] Aldrin joked to him. Armstrong turned to face the rear of the cabin, then lowered himself to the floor on his hands until he could kneel on it and put his lower legs out of the hatch.

"You want those bags?" Aldrin asked from inside the hatch.[11] What he was offering Armstrong was a jettison bag, for getting rid of garbage. It held empty food packages and beverage containers, and cartons that had held snacks. All this stuff weighed something, and every ounce of weight in a craft rising into orbit would use up some fuel. Armstrong took the bag from Aldrin, leaned over the edge of the platform known as the porch, and dropped the bag to the ground below.

Checking to make sure he was lined up with the hatch, he began to slide himself backward on his knees until he was far enough out to be able to stand upright on the porch outside the hatch. "Okay. Houston, I'm on the porch," Armstrong told Mission Control.[12]

Armstrong carefully started down the ladder. There was a television camera mounted on the LM, focused to show Armstrong as he stepped onto the Moon. It was showing his movement to what was later estimated to be more than six hundred million people watching on Earth.[13] "Okay. Neil, we can see you coming down the ladder now," said the voice from Mission Control.[14]

The bottom step on the ladder was about three feet up from the LM foot pad on the ground. When Armstrong reached it, he announced. "I'm at the foot of the ladder." He apparently felt he should describe what he saw as he looked down. "The LM footpads are only depressed in the surface about 1 or 2 inches, although the surface appears to be very, very fine grained, as you get close to it. It's almost like a powder."[15] He was letting his listeners know that even though the Moon soil was formed of a fine, powdery substance, it was obviously packed together hard enough to support the weight of the LM. "I'm going to step off the LM now," he told everyone, and did so.[16]

Armstrong had his right hand on the ladder and stepped down with his left foot. But he quickly brought his left foot up for a moment, then put it firmly down again. A moment later he put his right foot down beside it.

Chapter 8

The event that millions of people could only dream of over thousands of years of time had actually come true. There was a human standing on the Moon, almost a quarter of a million miles away from the world on which he been born.

A moment later, the millions watching the event on television heard his words. "That's one small step for man, one giant leap for mankind," he said.[1] Later, Armstrong stated that he had intended to say that it was "one small step for *a* man," which would have made the statement clearer. The footprint he had made stepping down from the ladder was a perfect imprint of the sole of his boot.

Collecting Rocks and Taking a Moon Jog

The first thing Armstrong was supposed to do when he stepped onto the Moon was to put some surface soil into a special bag. If the landing suddenly had to be cut short, there would be at least some material from the Moon for Earth's scientists to study. However, Armstrong wanted to take pictures so that people on Earth could see what the surface of the Moon looked like. With the camera mounted on the chest of his space suit, he snapped pictures until one of the men at Houston reminded him to collect the soil sample. He quickly reached into a pocket on his suit and

One of the first steps taken on the Moon, this is an image of Buzz Aldrin's bootprint from the *Apollo 11* mission.

pulled out the bag and a scoop. He filled the bag with powdery soil and several small rocks.

About fourteen minutes later, Aldrin joined Armstrong on the Moon. Before coming down, however, he apparently felt compelled to show off his sense of humor. "I want to back up and partially close the hatch," he told Armstrong. "Making sure not to lock it on my way out!"[2]

Armstrong chuckled. If Aldrin were to lock the hatch, there would be no way for the two men to get back into the LM. They would die on the Moon.

Standing on the Moon, Armstrong and Aldrin faced each other. They reached out and slapped each other on the shoulder. Then they peered about taking in the sights in all directions.

"Beautiful view!" Aldrin said.

"Isn't that something!" Armstrong agreed. "Magnificent sight out here."

"Magnificent desolation," Aldrin said.[3]

An ink-black sky extended in all directions. In the foreground, as far as the eye could see, the Moon's surface was completely covered with pieces of rock and small craters. To one side, some distance away, was what appeared to be the rim of a large crater.

Armstrong and Aldrin now began to gather rocks. Some time earlier, Aldrin had speculated on the possibility of discovering purple rocks on the Moon. It seemed to him that such an unearthly place might have some kind of truly unearthly rock, of an odd purplish color and a peculiar shine. Now he suddenly called out, "And Neil, didn't I say we might see some purple rocks?"

This is one of the Moon rocks Armstrong and Aldrin collected during the *Apollo 11* mission.

**Astronaut Buzz Aldrin
walks on the Moon.**

"Find a purple rock?" asked Armstrong.

"Yes," Aldrin claimed. "They are small, sparkly . . ."[4]

Armstrong grinned.

A Memorial That Will Last for Millions of Years

The two men then went to the LM and stood before it. Attached to the bottom was a metal plate engraved with a message that is a memorial to the Moon landing. The metal plate had been covered to protect it, and the two men uncovered it. Armstrong read the words aloud:

HERE MEN FROM THE PLANET EARTH
FIRST SET FOOT UPON THE MOON
JULY 1969, A.D.
WE CAME IN PEACE FOR ALL MANKIND[5]

The signatures of the *Apollo 11* crewmembers and of the U.S. President Richard M. Nixon were engraved on the plate beneath the message. When the two astronauts would go back up to *Columbia*, the memorial would be left behind. There would be no wind, rain, or polluted air to wear the message away.

One of the tasks Aldrin had been assigned was to

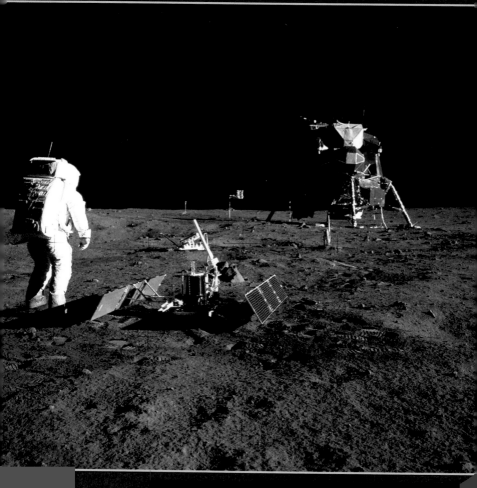

and found it a bit difficult at first. He had to be careful when he stopped or turned, or he was liable to fall down. However, he soon found that he had become used to things and could move quite easily.

While Armstrong scooped more Moon rocks and soil into special boxes, Aldrin set up the apparatus called a solar wind collector for the first of *Apollo 11*'s scientific experiments. Solar wind is a continuous flow of radiation and hot gases that come off the sun and rush through space at a speed of about 310 miles per second. The solar wind collector was a sheet of specially lined aluminum foil on a pole. It was put on the ground facing the sun, to catch the nuclei (centers) of gas atoms carried by solar wind. The nuclei captured by the aluminum foil would be of great value in helping scientists learn more about the structure of the sun. In one hour and seventeen minutes the foil collected 10 trillion atomic nuclei.[6] Then it was taken down, rolled up, and stored in one of the boxes of rocks. Eventually, it was brought to a laboratory on Earth for careful examination.

More Experiments and an American Flag on the Moon

While the solar wind collector was up, Aldrin set up the apparatus for the second experiment, called the passive seismic package. This was a device that could pick up vibrations caused by meteorites hitting the Moon's surface, or things happening inside the Moon,

Astronaut Buzz Aldrin walks on the lunar surface. In the right background is the *Eagle*. On the left is the solar wind collector. Armstrong took this photograph.

such as an earthquake (or rather, Moonquake) or volcanic activity. The passive seismic package was left in place when the astronauts left the Moon, and continued to send reports back to Earth for some time.

A third device was designed to pick up a laser beam fired from Earth and reflect it back. That would enable scientists to measure the distance of the Moon from Earth at that point in its orbit. It turned out to be 226,970.9 miles.[7]

Buzz Aldrin salutes the United States flag on the surface of the Moon.

Next came the ceremony of planting an American flag on the Moon. The flag would just hang motionless on the airless windless Moon, so it had been stiffened with a wire running along its upper edge, to make it appear as if it were flying. However, getting the flag to stand upright in the powdery dust that was the Moon's "soil" turned out to be very difficult. Armstrong and Aldrin had some bad moments fearing that the flag would topple over if they let go of it, which would be embarrassing. Finally they got the flagpole to stay upright in the powdery soil by pounding it down with the hammer they had brought for collecting rocks. Armstrong then took a picture of Aldrin saluting the flag.

Chapter 9

The time had come to end the "Moon walk." Armstrong, the first human to set foot on the surface of the Moon, had spent two hours and fourteen minutes there. Aldrin had been on the surface for just about one hour and forty-four minutes. Now, with Aldrin in the lead they clumped back up the ladder and wiggled their way through the hatch into the upper portion of the LM. They sealed the hatch and pressurized the cabin, filling it with oxygen. Then, in order to lighten the LM's load and help make the ascent easier, they disposed of everything that was no longer needed. They disconnected themselves from their bulky life-support backpacks, opened the hatch, and tossed them out onto the surface of the Moon. Next went the overshoes they had worn on the surface and all their empty, crumpled food packages.

At 12:54 in the afternoon, Houston time, *Eagle* departed from the Moon. Aldrin pressed the button for liftoff. *Eagle*'s upper portion blasted free, leaving the lower portion behind. It resembled a fat, four-legged spider squatting on the gray Moon landscape. Unlike the slow shuddering liftoff of a spacecraft on Earth, *Eagle*'s liftoff in the weak gravity of the Moon was like a sudden rush upward. Within moments the LM was rising at a rate of half a mile per second.[1]

HORNET + 3

President Richard M. Nixon welcomes the *Apollo 11* astronauts aboard the U.S.S. *Hornet*. Already confined to the Mobile Quarantine Facility are (left to right) Neil Armstrong, Michael Collins, and Edwin "Buzz" Aldrin, Jr.

the tunnel and entered *Columbia* through the air lock. They detached the tunnel and sealed the air lock. *Eagle* was now floating free in orbit over the Moon.

Some seven hours later, Michael Collins turned on the engine that pushed *Apollo 11* out of orbit and sent it on the three-day journey back to Earth. What many people thought, and still think, was that the greatest achievement in human history, was successfully concluded.

Messages of congratulations flooded into America from all over the world. There was one from the president of the Soviet Union, whose country had lost the moon race: "Congratulations and best wishes to the courageous space pilots."[3]

Most Americans, of course, were overwhelmed with pride and awe for what their country had accomplished. President Richard Nixon called the eight-day mission, "The greatest week in the history of the world since the Creation!"[4]

Apollo 11 returned to Earth on Thursday, July 24, 1969, at 1:16 P.M., Houston time. Upon being taken to the aircraft carrier *Hornet*, the astronauts were immediately put under quarantine in an aluminum trailer parked on the *Hornet*'s hangar deck. It was sealed tight and the astronauts were kept in quarantine for twenty-one days, the period of time it takes an Earth disease to reach a point when it can cause an epidemic. After that, the danger is over. In the meantime, the astronauts did their best

The Unimpressed, Uninterested, and Uncaring

Not everyone in America was favorably impressed by the Moon landing. The attitude of some people was that instead of spending hundreds of millions of dollars to get to the Moon, the government should have been doing something about poverty, unemployment, and racial problems in America, on Earth.

Despite watching it on television, some people believed that the Moon landing had never really even happened and had actually been staged somewhere. A newspaper reporter asked a New York City man for his opinion on this, and the man laughingly told him, "My wife, she says they're really not on the Moon at all, they're just somewhere in South Jersey."[6] Some people just could not believe that such a thing as space travel to the Moon was really possible.

Some people in other countries were not interested in the Moon landing. The famous artist Pablo Picasso said of the Moon landing, "It means nothing to me. I have no opinion about it, and I don't care."[7] Most people did not feel the way Picasso did, however.

to amuse themselves. They talked, played cards, and watched movies. However, when there were still a number of nights to go, Michael Collins said, plaintively, "I want out."[5]

For most people who saw men walking on the Moon, the Moon landing was tremendously important and exciting. It was the climax of a twenty-four-year period when what many people had believed to be impossible actually happened. Spaceships became a reality. Human beings actually went into space and did incredible, never-before-done things there. For many people, especially Americans, it was a thrilling, exciting time—a tremendous historical event to have lived through.

Chapter 10

Project Apollo was not finished. Nine more missions were scheduled. NASA scientists believed there was still information to find out about the Moon, and work to be done there.

Just about four months after the successful *Apollo 11* mission, *Apollo 12* was launched on November 14, 1969. Its crew was Charles "Pete" Conrad, Alan Bean, and Richard Gordon.

The *Apollo 12* crew had a special job. In 1966, the United States had sent a number of robotic spacecraft called Surveyors to the Moon. Bean and Conrad went down to the Moon's surface in the LM and landed as close to one of the Surveyors as they could get. They went out and removed several parts that scientists wanted brought back for study. The mission was an overwhelming success.

Apollo 13 was launched on April 11, 1970. Its commander was James Lovell and the other two crew members were John Swigert and Fred Haise.

The mission nearly became a disaster. About forty thousand miles from the Moon, there was an explosion in an oxygen tank in the Service Module, and oxygen leaked out into space. The Moon landing was cancelled and instead of beginning to circle the Moon in an orbit, *Apollo 13* headed

Crewmen aboard the U.S.S. *Iwo Jima*, prime recovery ship for the *Apollo 13* mission, hoist the Command Module aboard. The *Apollo 13* crewmen were already aboard *Iwo Jima* when this photograph was taken. The *Apollo 13* spacecraft splashed down at 12:07 P.M. April 17, 1970, in the South Pacific Ocean.

back toward Earth. It was a difficult and heroic return, but the spacecraft landed safely on April 17, 1970, and the world rejoiced that the crew had survived.

The Last Missions

NASA checked, investigated, and examined, until they were sure they knew what had happened to *Apollo 13*. It was more than ten months before they were ready to continue with the Apollo program. *Apollo 14* was launched on January 31, 1971, and was intended to do all the things the *Apollo 13* mission would have done. The crew was Alan Shepard, commander, who had been the first American to go into space, and Edgar Mitchell and Stuart Roosa.

The astronauts of the first three missions to make Moon landings had to walk to get to where they wanted to go on the Moon's surface. *Apollo 15* had a car. The mission launched on July 26, 1971, with a crew of three—David Scott, commander; James Irwin; and Al Worden. Their car was a battery-powered, four-wheeled vehicle known as a lunar roving vehicle. It could carry two men up to sixty miles at a speed of ten miles per hour. Having this vehicle enabled astronauts Scott and Irwin to explore a much greater area than had been possible before. *Apollo 16* launched on April 16, 1972, with John Young, Thomas Mattingly, and Charles Duke, Jr., and

The lunar roving vehicle (LRV) transported astronauts and materials on the Moon. An LRV was used on each of the last three Apollo missions, *Apollo 15*, *Apollo 16*, and *Apollo 17*. This photograph was taken during the *Apollo 15* mission in 1971.

Apollo 17, launched on December 7, 1972, with Harrison Schmitt, Ronald Evans, and Gene Cernan. Both of these missions also had a lunar roving vehicle.

Apollo 17 was the last manned Moon-landing mission to be launched. The men who landed on the Moon after the first Moon landing had done a lot of exploring and brought back a lot of rocks, but there were no new or major discoveries, as had been hoped for. Three more missions had been scheduled, but they were cancelled. The Apollo Project had ended.

What Does the Future Hold?

For a few years after the last manned Moon-landing mission, there was talk about activities that might be done on the Moon. Perhaps a station might be built there, from which spacecraft would be launched to explore Mars and the Moons of Jupiter and Saturn. There was talk of searching for resources on the Moon. Gradually, all such talk died away.

The 1960s were a time of tremendous discoveries and tremendous events in space, with America at the forefront. However, by the mid-1980s, America's goals for its role in space had changed, and some American astronauts[1] and space scientists[2] believed that the Soviet Union had become the world's leader in space technology and exploration. Today, America and Russia (formerly the main part of the Soviet Union), which were once competing against each other in the "space race," are now cooperating in the building of the International Space Station, which is expected to be finished in 2010.

Nearly half a century after the last Moon landing was made, Americans will hopefully again go to the Moon. Even now, NASA is working on a gigantic new space program known as the Constellation Program. A six-person spacecraft to be called *Orion*, is being designed and built. If all goes well, it will take people, machines, and supplies to the Moon in 2020. This will be the beginning of the building of a Moon base, from which craft could be launched to explore space. It is possible that many young people alive today will see a time when people are living and working on the Moon—and some young people of today may be among them.

TIMELINE

1945—May 2: Wernher von Braun turns himself and his entire staff of scientists and engineers over to American forces in Germany.

1957—October 4: The Soviet Union launches *Sputnik I.*

November 3: The Soviet Union launches *Sputnik 2,* containing a dog, Laika, the first animal to go into space.

1958—January 31: The United States launches into orbit a satellite called *Explorer 1.*

July 29: The U.S. Congress creates the National Aeronautics and Space Administration (NASA).

August: NASA begins to organize Project Mercury, a program for sending manned space crafts into space.

1959—September 14: An unmanned Soviet craft, *Luna 2,* crash-lands on the Moon, becoming the first craft from Earth to reach the surface of an object in space.

October 4: The unmanned Soviet craft *Luna 3* flies around the Moon taking photographs that are transmitted back to Earth. Some of these show the side of the Moon that has never before been seen by humans.

1961—April 12: Soviet cosmonaut Yuri Gagarin becomes the first human to go into space in a craft called *Vostok 1,* making a single orbit of Earth.

May 5: U.S. astronaut Alan Shepard becomes the first American in space.

May 25: In a televised speech to Congress, U.S. President John F. Kennedy announces that America intends to land a man on the Moon before the end of the decade.

July 21: U.S. astronaut Virgil Grissom in a Mercury craft named *Liberty Bell 7* makes a second suborbital flight.

1962—February 20: U.S. astronaut John Glenn makes a three-orbit spaceflight at a height of 163 miles in a Mercury spacecraft named *Friendship 7*.

1963—January: NASA begins a program to be called Project Gemini.

1965—March 18: In a two-man spacecraft called *Voskhod 2*, cosmonauts Alexei Leonov and Pavel Belyayev are launched into orbit. Leonov goes outside for ten minutes and makes the first "space walk."

June 3: Astronauts James McDivitt and Edward White are launched in a craft labeled *Gemini 5*. White leaves the craft and makes the first American "space walk."

December 15: A spacecraft labeled *Gemini 6-A* is launched into the same orbit as *Gemini 7*. The pilot, astronaut Walter Schirra moves his craft until its nose is only twelve inches from *Gemini 7* craft. This is a perfect rendezvous.

1966—March 16: An unmanned Agena spacecraft and a Gemini craft labeled *Gemini 8*, with astronauts Neil Armstrong and David Scott, are launched into the same orbit. Armstrong, the Gemini pilot, docks perfectly with the Agena.

1967—January 27: During a test of the *Apollo 1* spacecraft, a fire kills astronauts Virgil Grissom, Edward White, and Roger Chafee.

November 9: An unmanned, redesigned Apollo command module labeled *Apollo 4*, is launched into orbit by a Saturn V rocket.

1968—January 22: Another unmanned Apollo command module, *Apollo 5*, is launched into orbit.

October 11: *Apollo 7* becomes the first manned Apollo mission, with a crew of Walter Schirra, Walter Cunningham, and Donn Eisele.

December 21: *Apollo 8*, with a crew of Frank Borman, James Lovell, Jr., and William Anders, becomes the first spacecraft to carry humans to an orbit around the Moon.

1969—March 3: *Apollo 9*, with a crew of James McDivitt, David Scott, and Russell Schweickart, is launched into Earth orbit to test operation of the command/service module (CSM) and lunar module (LM).

May 18: *Apollo 10* is launched to the Moon, with a crew of Eugene Cernan, John Young, and Thomas Stafford. With the CSM in lunar orbit, the LM makes a flight down to about nine miles above the Moon's surface. Then it returns and docks with the CSM.

July 4: A fuel explosion destroys a Soviet rocket. The Soviet Union is forced out of the "Moon Race."

July 16: *Apollo 11* lifts off for the Moon. The crew is Neil Armstrong, Michael Collins, and Buzz Aldrin.

July 20: *Apollo 11*'s LM, carrying Neil Armstrong and Buzz Aldrin, lands on the surface of the Moon. Armstrong leaves the LM and steps off the ladder. For the first time, a man stands on the Moon.

CHAPTER NOTES

Chapter 1. The Dream of Visiting the Moon

1. David A. Clary, *Rocket Man* (New York: Hyperion, 2003), p. 122.

2. John W. R. Taylor, *Rockets and Missiles* (New York: Grosset & Dunlap, 1970), p. 17.

Chapter 2. The Weapon That Became a Spacecraft

1. *American Heritage Picture History of World War II* (American Heritage Publishing Co., 1966), p. 507.

2. Winston S. Churchill, *The Second World War, Volume II* (New York: Time Incorporated, 1960), p. 416.

3. Buzz Aldrin and Malcolm McConnell, *Men From Earth* (New York: Bantam Books,1989), p. 23.

4. *Chicago Daily News*, October 5, 1957, p. 1.

5. Ibid.

6. Ibid.

7. Dr. David Whitehouse, "First Dog in Space Died Within Hours," *BBC News*, October 28, 2002 <http://news.bbc.co.uk/2/hi/sci/tech/2367681.stm> (January 7, 2008).

8. "Explorer 1 First U.S. Satellite: History," *NASA Jet Propulsion Laboratory*, January, 31, 2003 <http://www.jpl.nasa.gov/explorer/history/> (January 7, 2008).

9. Ibid.

10. Aldrin and McConnell, p. 20.

Chapter 3. America Begins Its Space Program

1. John W. R. Taylor, *Rockets and Missiles* (New York: Grosset & Dunlap, 1970), p. 110.

2. Buzz Aldrin and Malcolm McConnell, *Men From Earth* (New York: Bantam Books, 1989), p. 47.

3. Peter Bond, *Heroes In Space: From Gagarin to Challenger* (Oxford: Basil Blackwell, Ltd., 1987), p. 15.

4. Ibid.

5. Aldrin and McConnell, p. 66.

6. Ibid.

7. David West Reynolds, *Apollo, The Epic Journey to the Moon* (New York: Harcourt, Inc., 2002), p. 42.

8. Bond, p. 34.

9. Ibid., p. 41.

10. Ibid., p. 42.

Chapter 4. Solving the Problems of a Moon Landing

1. Donald K. "Deke" Slayton with Michael Cassutt, *Deke!* (New York: Forge, 1994), p. 127.

2. Peter Bond, *Heroes In Space: From Gagarin to Challenger* (Oxford: Basil Blackwell, Ltd., 1987), p. 77.

3. Mary C. White, "Detailed Biographies of Apollo I Crew—Ed White," *NASA History*, August 4, 2006, <http://history.nasa.gov/Apollo204/zorn/white.htm> (January 3, 2007).

4. "50 Years of the Space Age: Gemini IV Umbilical," *National Air and Space Museum*, © 2007, <http://www.nasm.si.edu/events/spaceage/geminiumb.htm> (January 3, 2007).

5. Bond, p. 107.

6. Buzz Aldrin and Malcolm McConnell, *Men From Earth* (New York: Bantam Books, 1989), p. 139.

Chapter 5. The "Moon Race" Begins

1. Buzz Aldrin and Malcolm McConnell, *Men From Earth* (New York: Bantam Books, 1989), p. 175.

2. Rod Pyle, *Destination Moon* (New York: Collins, 2005), p. 18.

3. Andrew Chaikin, *A Man on the Moon, The Voyages of the Apollo Astronauts* (New York: Viking, 1994), p. 17.

4. Aldrin and McConnell, p. 79.

Chapter 6. Checking Out the Moon

1. Andrew Chaikin, *A Man on the Moon, The Voyages of the Apollo Astronauts* (New York: Viking, 1994), p. 90.

2. Ibid., p. 119.

3. Ibid., p. 141.

4. Ibid., p. 159.

5. Buzz Aldrin and Malcolm McConnell, *Men From Earth* (New York: Bantam Books, 1989), p. 220.

6. David West Reynolds, *Apollo, The Epic Journey to the Moon* (New York: Harcourt, Inc., 2002), p. 128.

Chapter 7. The First Man on the Moon

1. NASA, *Apollo 11 Spacecraft Commentary*, p. 13, July 16–24, 1969, <http://www.jsc.nasa.gov/history/mission_trans/AS11_PAO.PDF> (December 12, 2007).

2. NASA, "Apollo 11 Mission Commentary," *Apollo 11 (PAO) Spacecraft Commentary*, July 20, 1969, <http://history.nasa.gov/alsj/a11/a11transcript_pao.htm> (December 12, 2007).

3. Buzz Aldrin and Malcolm McConnell, *Men From Earth* (New York: Bantam Books, 1989), p. 234.

4. NASA, "Apollo 11 Mission Commentary."

5. Ibid.

6. Ibid.

7. Ibid.

8. Ibid.

9. Aldrin and McConnell, p. 240.

10. NASA, *Apollo 11 Technical Air-to-Ground Transcript*, n.d., <http://www.history.nasa.gov/alsj/a11/a11transcript_tec.html> (December 12, 2007).

11. Ibid.

12. Ibid.

13. Andrew Chaikin, *A Man on the Moon, The Voyages of the Apollo Astronauts* (New York: Viking, 1994), p. 213.

14. NASA, *Apollo 11 Technical Air-to-Ground Transcript*.

15. Ibid.

16. Ibid.

Chapter 8. Earthlings on the Moon

1. NASA, *Apollo 11 Technical Air-to-Ground Transcript*, n.d., <http://www.history.nasa.gov/alsj/a11/a11transcript_tec.html> (December 12, 2007).

2. Ibid.

3. Ibid.

4. Ibid.

5. Ibid.

6. "Men on the Moon," *LIFE Magazine*, August 8, 1969, p. 25.

7. Neil Armstrong, Michael Collins, Edwin R. Aldrin, Jr., with Gene Farmer and Dora Jane Hamblin, *First on the Moon* (Boston: Little, Brown and Company, 1970), p. 432.

Chapter 9. The Dream That Came True

1. Buzz Aldrin and Malcolm McConnell, *Men From Earth* (New York: Bantam Books, 1989), p. 244.

2. Andrew Chaikin, *A Man on the Moon, The Voyages of the Apollo Astronauts* (New York: Viking, 1994), p. 280.

3. Aldrin and McConnell, p. 222.

4. *This Fabulous Century, 1960–1970* (New York: Time-Life Books, 1972), p. 280.

5. "The Apollo Years," *Canada's Aerospace Medicine Pioneers*, August 18, 2006, <http://www.space.gc.ca/asc/eng/astronauts/osm_carpentier.asp> (December 12, 2007).

6. *This Fabulous Century, 1960–1970*, p. 273.

7. Ibid., p. 280.

Chapter 10. The Return to the Moon

1. Buzz Aldrin and Malcolm McConnell, *Men From Earth* (New York: Bantam Books, 1989), p. 253.

2. Bruce Murray, *Journey Into Space* (New York: W. W. Norton Company, 1989), p. 23.

GLOSSARY

aeronautics—The design, construction, and operation of aircraft.

atmosphere—A layer of gas or gases, such as those forming Earth's air, that may surround a planet or natural satellite, such as the Moon, held in place by gravity.

capsule—An early form of spacecraft.

centrifuge—A machine consisting of a compartment at the end of a long shaft that spins at great speed around a central point.

ejection—Being very quickly thrown out of a vehicle or enclosure.

hysteria—A state of being unable to control emotions; experiencing such extreme fear, panic, or grief that the body and brain no longer work properly.

luminescent—Giving off glowing light without much heat.

manual control—Operated by a human rather than a computer.

module—A part that when put together with other parts forms a vehicle or machine.

radiation—Energy in the form of waves or particles that can often be harmful.

suborbital—A spaceflight that does not get high enough to enter orbit

velocity—Speed of an object in motion.

FURTHER READING

Ackroyd, Peter. *Escape From Earth*. New York: DK Pub., 2003.

Asimov, Isaac. *Global Space Programs*. Milwaukee, Wisc.: Gareth Stevens Pub., 2006.

Harland, David M. *How NASA Learned to Fly in Space: An Exciting Account of the Gemini Missions*. Burlington, Ont.: Apogee Books, 2004.

Malam, John. *Man Walks on the Moon*. Mankato, Minn.: Smart Apple Media, 2003.

Mason, Paul. *The Moon Landing, July 20, 1969*. Orlando, Fla.: Raintree Steck-Vaughn, 2002.

McCutcheon, Bobbi and Scott McCutcheon. *Space and Astronomy: The People Behind the Science*. New York: Chelsea House, 2006.

Thimmesh, Catherine. *Team Moon: How 400,000 People Landed Apollo 11 on the Moon*. Boston: Houghton Mifflin Co., 2006.

INTERNET ADDRESSES

**Smithsonian National Air and Space Museum—
    Apollo 11**
<http://www.nasm.si.edu/collections/imagery/Apollo/
    AS11/a11.htm>

**Smithsonian National Air and Space Museum—
    The Apollo Program**
<http://www.nasm.si.edu/collections/imagery/Apollo/
    apollo.htm>

**Smithsonian National Air and Space Museum—
    Space Race**
<http://www.nasm.si.edu/exhibitions/gal114/SpaceRace/
    sec100/sec100.htm>

Index